The
Parallel Curriculum
in the Classroom
Book 1

With gratitude to the educators whose interest in the Parallel Curriculum Model has provided an impetus to explore its possibilities further, whose questions have caused us to deepen our thinking, and whose work in schools and classrooms has given legs to curriculum dreams.

The
Parallel Curriculum
in the Classroom
Book 1

Essays for Application Across the Content Areas K-12

A Joint Publication With the
National Association for Gifted Children

Carol Ann Tomlinson ◆ Sandra N. Kaplan ◆ Jeanne H. Purcell
Jann H. Leppien ◆ Deborah E. Burns ◆ Cindy A. Strickland

CORWIN PRESS
A SAGE Publications Company
Thousand Oaks, California

For information:

Corwin Press
A Sage Publications Company
2455 Teller Road
Thousand Oaks, California 91320
E-mail: order@corwinpress.com

Sage Publications Ltd.
1 Oliver's Yard
55 City Road
London EC1Y 1SP
United Kingdom

Sage Publications India Pvt. Ltd.
B-42, Panchsheel Enclave
Post Box 4109
New Delhi 110 017 India

Printed in the United States of America.

Library of Congress Cataloging-in-Publication Data

The parallel curriculum in the classroom / Carol Ann Tomlinson . . . [et al.].
    2 v. cm.
"A Joint Publication of the National Association for Gifted Children and Corwin Press."
Includes bibliographical references and index.
Contents: bk. 1. Essays for application across the content areas, K-12 — bk. 2. Units for application across the content areas, K-12.
ISBN 0-7619-2971-1 (cloth : v. 1) — ISBN 0-7619-2972-X (pbk. : v. 1) — ISBN 1-4129-2527-4 (cloth : v. 2) — ISBN 1-4129-2528-2 (pbk. : v. 2)
    1. Gifted children—Education—Curricula.
2. Curriculum planning. I. Tomlinson, Carol A. II. National Association for Gifted Children (U.S.)
LC3993.2.P344 2006
371.95′3—dc22

                                                2005007504

This book is printed on acid-free paper.

05 06 07 08 09 10 9 8 7 6 5 4 3 2 1

Acquisitions Editor:	Robert D. Clouse
Editorial Assistant:	Jingle Vea
Project Editor:	Tracy Alpern
Copy Editor:	Mary L. Tederstrom
Proofreader:	Annette Pagliaro
Typesetter:	C&M Digitals (P) Ltd.
Indexer:	Sylvia Coates
Cover Designer:	Michael Dubowe

Contents

Acknowledgments

Corwin Press gratefully acknowledges the contributions of the following manuscript reviewers:

Sherri S. Jarrett
GATE Resource Specialist
Peter Muhlenberg Middle School
Woodstock, VA

Sandy Marzec
GATE Teacher
Twin Lakes Elementary School
Federal Way, WA

Pamela Lyle-Walton
GATE Teacher
Nautilus Elementary School
Federal Way, WA

Kathleen M. Pierce
Assistant Professor
Graduate Department of
   Education & Human Services
Rider University
Lawrenceville, NJ

Gillian I. Eriksson Sluti
Instructor
Educational Studies, College of
   Education
University of Central Florida
Orlando, FL

Vicki Vaughn
Instructor of G/T Grad Courses
Codirector of Gifted/Talented
   Licensure
Purdue University
West Lafayette, IN

Marsha Sobel
Executive Director, Curriculum
   and Instruction
Newburgh Enlarged City
   School District
Newburgh, NY

About the Authors

Carol Ann Tomlinson's career as an educator encompasses 21 years as a public school teacher, including 12 years as a program administrator of special services for struggling and advanced learners. She was Virginia's Teacher of the Year in 1974. More recently, she has been a faculty member at the University of Virginia's Curry School of Education, where she is currently Professor of Educational Leadership, Foundations, and Policy and was named Outstanding Professor in 2004. Also at the University of Virginia she is codirector of the university's Summer Institute on Academic Diversity. She is author of more than 150 books, articles, and chapters on differentiation and curriculum.

Sandra N. Kaplan has been a teacher and administrator of gifted programs in an urban school district in California. Currently, she is Clinical Professor in Learning and Instruction at the University of Southern California's Rossier School of Education. She has authored articles and books on the nature and scope of differentiated curriculum for gifted students. Her primary area of concern is modifying the core and differentiated curriculum to meet the needs of inner-city and urban gifted learners. She is a past president of the California Association for the Gifted (CAG) and the National Association for Gifted Children (NAGC). She has been nationally recognized for her contributions to gifted education.

Jeanne H. Purcell is the consultant to the Connecticut State Department of Education for gifted and talented education. Prior to her work there, she was an administrator for Rocky Hill Public Schools, where she coordinated a staff-development initiative on curriculum differentiation; a program specialist with the National Research Center on the Gifted and Talented (NRC/GT), where she worked collaboratively with other researchers on national issues related to high-achieving young people; an instructor of Teaching the Talented, a graduate-level program in gifted education; and a staff developer to school districts across the country and Canada. She has been an English teacher, community service coordinator, and teacher of the gifted, K–12, for 18 years in Connecticut school districts. She is the author of two books and has published many articles that have appeared in *Educational Leadership, Gifted Child*

Quarterly, Roeper Review, Educational and Psychological Measurement, National Association of Secondary School Principals' Bulletin, Our Children: The National PTA Magazine, Parenting for High Potential, and *Journal for the Education of the Gifted.* She is active in her local community and in the National Association for Gifted Children (NAGC) as a member of the executive board and board of directors. She served on the awards committee and the curriculum committee where she cochaired the annual Curriculum Awards competition.

Jann H. Leppien is an associate professor at the University of Great Falls in Great Falls, Montana, where she teaches coursework in curriculum and instruction, gifted education, assessment and learning, educational research, and methods in social sciences. In addition, she teaches curriculum courses and thinking skills courses online and in the Three Summers program at the University of Connecticut. Before joining the faculty at the University of Great Falls, she worked as a research assistant for The National Research Center on the Gifted and Talented (NRC/GT). She has been a classroom teacher, enrichment specialist, and coordinator of a gifted education program in Montana. She is the coauthor of *The Multiple Menu Model: A Practical Guide for Developing Differentiated Curriculum* and *The Parallel Curriculum: A Design to Develop High Potential and Challenge High-Ability Students.* She conducts workshops for teachers in the areas of differentiated instruction, curriculum design and assessment, thinking skills, and program development. She has served on the board of the National Association for Gifted Children (NAGC) and currently serves on the Association for the Education of Gifted Underachieving Students (AEGUS).

Deborah E. Burns is a curriculum coordinator for the Cheshire, Connecticut, schools. Previously, she worked for 15 years as an associate professor and an administrator in educational psychology at the University of Connecticut, where she taught courses in curriculum design, differentiation, assessment, talent development, and thinking skills instruction. Her related professional experience includes K–8 classroom teaching, work as a gifted education specialist, and work as a remedial reading and math specialist. As a consultant and program evaluator, she works with school districts nationwide. Her publications include journal articles, chapters, and books based on her research and work with teachers and in classrooms. She graduated from Michigan State University in 1973 with her BS, from Ashland University in 1978 with a MEd, and from the University of Connecticut in 1987 with her PhD.

 **Cindy A. Strickland** is currently pursuing her doctorate in Educational Psychology with an emphasis in gifted education at the University of Virginia, where she serves as teaching assistant to Carol Ann Tomlinson. She is an international consultant in the areas of differentiation of instruction, the Parallel Curriculum Model, and gifted education. Her publications include *Differentiation in Practice: A Resource Guide for Differentiating Curriculum, Grades 9–12* and *In Search of the Dream: Designing Schools and Classrooms That Work for High Potential Students From Diverse Cultural Backgrounds*. She has been a teacher for more than 20 years. She has taught music, French, humanities, and gifted education to elementary through college-age students.

Introducing the Parallel Curriculum Model in the Classroom

Carol Ann Tomlinson and Sandra N. Kaplan

When *The Parallel Curriculum: A Design to Develop High Potential and Challenge High-Ability Learners* was published (Tomlinson et al., 2002), the six of us who had authored it already knew *we* found the ideas in the model to be both interesting and challenging. We already knew *we* were more effective as educators and as individuals as a result of the collaboration that had led to the model and its publication. What we did not know was the degree to which others might share these opinions.

Since the initial book was released, we've discovered at least two things. First, we were not finished with the Parallel Curriculum Model (PCM); we were just beginning. Second, the collaboration we were about to begin with other educators would be far more multifaceted and fulfilling even than the collaboration we had shared among ourselves.

In the three years since the model's initial publication, we have provided professional development opportunities on the model for hundreds of educators in locations around the country. We have talked with educators from other countries about using the model in their schools. We have taught university courses on the model. We have worked with excellent professionals as they developed units based on the model. We have established a Web site on the model (www.nagc.org/pcmlearning/pcmindex.html). We have provided initial distance learning opportunities on the model. We have developed a brief video. In general, our days in those intervening three years have been permeated with thoughts about the PCM. Most of our thinking has been fueled by the opportunity to share ideas about the model with other educators. As is always the case in education, whenever we set out to be teachers, we learned from those we hoped to teach. This book is an extension of the conversations we have shared—individually and as a group—with educators who made *us* proud to be educators.

ABOUT THE BOOK

The Parallel Curriculum Model in the Classroom is published in two books. This first book includes five essays by the authors of the PCM that are intended to clarify and expand upon the model. The second book contains eight units that apply the PCM in varied subjects and at varied grade levels. The two books can stand alone, but they are designed to work in tandem to extend a reader's understanding of the PCM and to illustrate some ways in which the model can be used in classrooms.

The Essays

The essays in Book 1 are designed to further develop key ideas from *The Parallel Curriculum* (Tomlinson et al., 2002). First, Deborah Burns has developed a thoughtful, experience-based guide to writing units using the framework of the model. It is valuable for its clarity, but more so because it is derived from the journey of a stellar group of educators who have worked over a period of months to develop units based on the PCM. The PCM is a heuristic, not an algorithm. That is, the model provides guidelines for developing rich curriculum—it does not pretend to be a recipe or fill-in-the-template approach to curriculum design. For that reason, developing units with the PCM is a journey of thought—often nonlinear, recursive, reflective, and self-corrective.

To read about the experiences—insights and brick walls—of a group of high-quality educators as they applied the model is something like looking into our own minds through a mirror of shared experience. "I've done that," we say. "I got hung up there too." "Oh, now I see how I can tackle that issue." The PCM authors share the common belief that curriculum design and curriculum writing are as much about shaping the teacher as about shaping students for whom the curriculum is intended. Burns's essay demonstrates the power of that shaping process—and provides reassurance about the process as well.

Second, Jann Leppien writes about the potency of the questions that are a part of each of the model's four parallels. The four sets of focusing questions define the intent of the parallels in important ways. They provide curriculum developers with a reliable way to ensure that discussions, activities, presentations, products, and assessments achieve direction, meaning, and challenge. They are heuristics or guides that enable teachers to modify existing curriculum in ways that are likely to deepen its relevance for students and evoke new levels of thought in students. Leppien's essay is important in articulating the potency of the questions as educational tools.

Third, Sandra Kaplan takes us back to a critical premise of the model by discussing the importance of ensuring that students have substantial opportunities to work in all four of the model's parallels. The PCM is something like a camera with interchangeable lenses. The advantage of such a camera is that it allows both the photographer and the viewer of photographs to see the world reflected in a variety of ways. There would be little reason to purchase such a camera unless the photographer intended over time to change lenses as need and opportunity suggest. Similarly, the PCM offers teachers and students four ways to look at the world they study. Much of the model's power comes from its capacity to help students learn from multiple perspectives. Kaplan's case for using all the camera's lenses is a reminder of that potential for implementers of the model.

Fourth, Jeanne Purcell's essay expands our understanding of the most unique of the model's four parallels—the Curriculum of Identity. She reminds us that the best teaching has a payoff for the teacher as well as for the student. She also does vital work in delineating what the Curriculum of Identity is and what it is not. She makes clear that this parallel is not career guidance, an exploration of learning style, or an examination of general likes and dislikes. Rather, it asks students to examine the work of those deeply invested in the discipline and to learn about the nature of the discipline as well as what the work of experts reveals about the students' own dreams, values, modes of working, willingness to take risks or to contribute, and so on. Alternatively, the Curriculum of Identity asks students to study core concepts and principles central to a topic and to reflect on the power of those concepts and principles to uncover meaning in their lives. To achieve the intent of the Curriculum of Identity, Purcell reminds us, we must be clear on what the parallel intends and what it does not.

Last, Carol Tomlinson, Sandra Kaplan, and Kelly Hedrick write about the concept of Ascending Intellectual Demand (AID). Another unique contribution of the PCM model, AID is a heuristic or guide for thinking about what it means to provide continually escalating challenges for learners—including those who readily surpass our expectations in the classroom. This chapter expands on routes to AID. For example, AID reflects the nature and intent of the parallel(s) in which it is incorporated. That is, when students are engaging in study via the Curriculum of Connections, for instance, and need challenge beyond the parameters of the baseline curriculum, AID would be used to help students explore connections more rigorously. To that end, each of the four parallels offers questions designed to foster AID in that parallel. Those questions are valuable as ready mechanisms to help teachers provide challenge. They also serve as models for teachers who want to develop additional questions likely to evoke challenge.

Another route to AID can be envisioned as a progression toward expertise. This chapter provides general descriptions of how that progression may evolve as well as descriptions of movement toward expertise in math, science, language arts, and social studies—again giving teachers a useful starting point for thinking about this key element of the model, which cuts across all four parallels.

The Units

Book 2 presents eight curriculum units that were designed using the PCM. We have made a special effort to link the PCM information and guidelines in Book 1 with the creation of the exemplary units. However, we do not envision the units as off-the-shelf selections a teacher would pick up and teach. Rather, we believe that they will facilitate educators to better prepare effective, quality units of their own, especially those incorporating the PCM. A more detailed explanation of the rationale, methods, and resources used in the development of this PCM curriculum material is given in the Introduction to Book 2.

USING THE MODEL AND UNITS
FOR PROFESSIONAL DEVELOPMENT

To maximize the usefulness of the PCM and the units and essays included in Book 1 and Book 2, we suggest the following guidelines for professional development based on the model. The guidelines should help you ensure the integrity of the model and maximize the likelihood that work produced using the model addresses the intellectual needs of the students the model was designed to serve. We include the following points here, as well as in the second book, so that readers of Book 1 may begin immediately to contemplate what we consider the important steps in organizing classroom curriculum according to the PCM:

• Study the PCM (see *The Parallel Curriculum*, Tomlinson et al., 2002) to ensure that educators understand its philosophy and intent.

• Examine this model in comparison with other curriculum models. It is often through such a comparison that the value of a particular design becomes clear.

• Discuss the relationship between the PCM and current issues in both general and gifted education. Among those issues might be the changing nature of student populations, the evolving and expanding understanding of intelligence, the need to have many students exposed to high-quality curriculum, the possibility that high-quality curriculum can be a catalyst for both identifying and developing potential in learners, the need to balance equity and excellence in our schools, and the need to develop standards-based curriculum that honors our best knowledge about dynamic teaching and learning.

• Demonstrate learning experiences based on the PCM as a preface to using the model to develop curriculum for larger groups of students. Observing the model in practice is likely to be far more powerful than only reading or hearing about it.

• Propose a set of criteria to ensure that the integrity of the model is maintained as curriculum is developed. Such a list should help curriculum implementers make sure that their work is synchronized with the intent of the various parallels and the model as a whole. Just as stages of review accompany the process of writing for publication, reviews in the curriculum writing and implementation process need to precede "publication" for one or many groups of students.

• Field test units developed with the PCM. For example, two teachers might design a unit together. They may then try out the unit with their students and compare responses of students during the unit as well as examine student products from the unit. It is then possible for the two teachers to engage in a grounded discussion about the degree to which the unit seemed to facilitate student attainment of goals reflected in the unit and the model.

• Create a systematic plan to review PCM-based work in a school or district. This is likely to be most useful if done intermittently throughout the year so that in-process adjustments are possible.

• Develop a plan for disseminating the newly designed curriculum that includes ample opportunity for teachers who will use the curriculum to understand the PCM and the intent of the authors. Teachers at all levels of familiarity with PCM also need ample opportunity to ask questions about the implementation and refinement of the curriculum.

• Develop a plan to ensure that a wide range of stakeholders understands the model and benefits of using it with a wide range of learners. Helping teachers, administrators, parents, and community members understand and appreciate the goals and potential benefits of the model is paramount to the application and efficacy of the model and curriculum developed using the model.

In sum, the goal of the essays in Book 1 is to help educators think more fully and deeply about some important facets and "nonnegotiables" of the model, about the curriculum development process itself, and about diverse groups of students who would benefit from consistent work with rich, multifaceted, expert-oriented curriculum. In the end, it is our hope that the essays will guide classroom application of the PCM in ways that develop teachers and students who find pleasure in thought and growth.

In Praise
of Protocols

Navigating the Design Process Within
the Parallel Curriculum Model

Deborah E. Burns

One day last autumn, I spent about eight hours in the library of a public high school meeting with two groups of teachers and administrators who wanted to talk about curriculum, what made it exemplary, and how to design it to support thought-provoking learning for their students. By midday, I found myself with a little spare time as I waited for a second group to arrive. To stretch my legs, I roamed the rows and shelves of the library and soon spotted a book that piqued my curiosity. It was a reference book that explained the historical origins of many contemporary words and phrases. For my own amusement, I decided to find out if the book contained the word *curriculum*. Sure enough, the word has had a very rich history. With the initiation of the Parallel Curriculum Model (PCM), the word will surely have an even more interesting future.

CURRICULUM AS A ROAD MAP

The earliest meaning of the word *curriculum*, "a messenger's running course," can be traced to ancient Roman times. Later, in the 17th century, the word's meaning was transformed by the Scots to describe a different kind of course, "a carriage way or roadway." By 1904, the word *curriculum* appears to have changed its meaning once again, this time by users in the United States, to indicate "a student's course of study." Then, in the 1940s, the word's meaning evolved again, to connote "a plan of study for a given subject area or grade level." This explanation continues as our contemporary definition of the term.

It is interesting to consider how the historical meaning of the word *curriculum* continues to influence our contemporary perceptions and usage. As a metaphor, the notion of curriculum as a roadway for a learning journey provokes intriguing questions. Who are the travelers? What is their destination? Can different travelers have different destinations? Who prepares the map for the journey, and how do they create it? Who uses the map, and what do the travelers need to realize a successful journey?

This metaphor also helps us define our roles as curriculum writers and teachers. Depending on which role we assume, we might act as curriculum cartographers who create the road map and plan for student learning. Or, as teachers, we might serve as travel guides who use a curriculum road map to lead students along their learning journey. Both roles demand that we understand our learners, the learning process, and the kind of knowledge we want students to acquire as a result of their learning journey.

THE PURPOSE, PROBLEMS, AND PROCESS OF CURRICULUM WRITING

Most of us acknowledge that a curriculum plan is important. It confirms and communicates our learning objectives, ensures the proper integration and configuration of the various curriculum components, and ensures the alignment of content across grade levels, classrooms, and related topics in the same subject area.

However, there is a big difference between using a curriculum map created by someone else and being the cartographer who maps the way for others. Curriculum writing, like the mapping and planning process, is hard work. It requires time, patience, collaboration, research, dialogue, experimentation, reflection, revision, and a willingness to resist premature closure.

The mission of creating units based on the PCM, units that focus on discipline-based content; topic, time, or cultural connections; authentic practices and applications; or personal identity, is tantalizing and promises to make the hard work worthwhile. PCM also promises the opportunity to provide side trips during the learning journey to address differences in students' levels of expertise as well as their personal strengths and interests. But how do we go about drawing a better plan and map, based on the PCM, that supports the learner's journey to new and more challenging destinations?

THE GOAL AND SEQUENCE OF THIS ESSAY

This essay shares a process and protocol for writing PCM curriculum that evolved during the course of a yearlong project. The effort involved more than 40 different classroom teachers, gifted education specialists, administrators, university professors, and state department of education consultants from around the country. Working individually, in pairs, and in small groups, these educators were charged with the development of 24 different PCM curriculum units in science and social studies for students from varying socioeconomic and achievement levels.

Our long-term collaboration provided an ideal opportunity to observe, reflect upon, and describe the PCM design process. In addition, this partnership helped us articulate a common vision for PCM curricula, clarify the guiding questions we posed to ourselves during the process, identify the sequence of steps that appear to be most effective, and develop graphic organizers and templates to support the design process and communicate effectively with each other during that process. This essay shares these templates, procedures, and processes with others in an attempt to make the PCM curriculum writing process easier to organize and accomplish.

I begin the description of the design process with a discussion of the key components that are part of a curriculum plan. I also emphasize the reasons why educators need to articulate the first component—content and learning goals—from the start. Next, I consider the importance of modifying, aligning, and combining all the components to suit the unique purposes of each of the parallels in the PCM. Third, I investigate the definition of a protocol and a template and examine their purpose, usefulness, and constraints.

In the last two-thirds of this essay, readers will encounter a detailed explanation of the ten steps (or protocol) that most of our author cadre appeared to use in creating the PCM curriculum units. This protocol begins with three steps that helped our cadre of authors identify, categorize, and sequence the content goals for a PCM unit. The fourth step in the process involves the identification of the major segues within the unit and the time parameters for each section. Fifth, authors identify the appropriate teaching and learning activities, resources, and student products. Sixth, authors share focusing questions and the graphic organizers that helped them develop a learner profile and create appropriate opportunities for Ascending Intellectual Demand (AID). The seventh step provides an opportunity to explore the relationships among student products, rubrics, AID, and assessment. The eighth step reconsiders choice of content, tasks, time allocations, and related parallels in order to ensure alignment and make appropriate modifications. In the ninth step, readers review a graphic organizer useful in making decisions about what to include in an effective introduction to the unit. At the conclusion of these steps, or decision-making points, our cadre was ready to begin the tenth step, writing the actual lesson plans for their respective PCM units. The last section of this essay contains the templates and graphic organizers they used to develop the plans.

The set of steps for the PCM design process described in this essay was common to most of the authors in our project. To date, the strategies and protocols they used have been successful in supporting the work of other PCM authors, even though some authors skip steps or use the steps in a different order. The protocol I describe in this essay is by no means the only way to organize the common work of a group of authors or to design PCM curricula. It is likely that other groups, working within a different organizational structure or school culture, have developed or will continue to develop alternate methods that are just as effective or more comprehensive. We invite their collaboration and willingness to share their work. Their creativity and alternate perspectives deepen our understandings about PCM, its numerous facets, and its unexplored avenues and possibilities.

COMPONENTS OF A CURRICULUM PLAN

All curriculum units, those based on the PCM or any other model, can include a number of key features that support student learning. To be useful, even a basic curriculum guide must include *content standards* that students are to acquire and the topics or examples they will use to learn the content, *time allocations* needed to accomplish the learning, and *assessment systems* to track student progress and learning from the beginning to the end of the curriculum unit. In writing the Parallel Curriculum, we determined that a more comprehensive curriculum guide should include the components listed in Figure 1.1.

We quickly discovered that one of the possible components, the *content* we want students to learn and be able to apply, was the most important component for our decision making and planning. Comparable to the learner's or traveler's destination on a curriculum map, the *nature of that content* (e.g., facts, concepts, generalizations, principles, skills, attitudes, or applications) and the *relative importance of each kind of knowledge* addressed in the unit determine the use of one or more of the PCM parallels and, as a result, the unique configuration of the other elements that support the acquisition of this content knowledge. We explore the alternatives for selecting content in the first three steps of the writing protocol that follows.

THE CHALLENGE OF WRITING WELL-ALIGNED PARALLEL CURRICULUM MODEL CURRICULA

But designing PCM units, or any other kind of curriculum, is more than naming the content students are to learn. The following metaphor illustrates this basic understanding.

Like a list of food items needed to create a particular dish, the curriculum components act as the raw ingredients necessary to prepare and "serve" a particular lesson within a curriculum unit. There is, however, all the difference in the world between a pile of groceries sitting on a kitchen counter and a flavorful and nutritious dish served hot from the oven. To obtain the latter, the skillful cook must carefully choose the freshest and most appropriate ingredients, blend them together in just the right proportions, and apply heat energy to transform the uncooked ingredients into a satisfying, nourishing meal.

Likewise, the curriculum developer must carefully choose the ingredients of the lesson, combine them just so, and then apply the energy needed to transform the lessons into truly powerful learning experiences. Certainly, appealing to students' imagination and recognizing and attending to their prior knowledge by making the learning journey and content relevant to their individual lives is one way to capture this energy. Other methods involve the use of constructivist teaching and learning methods, the use of authentic resources and assignments, and the guarantee of appropriate levels of challenge for all students. All of these expectations are inherent in the design process for any of the PCM parallels (see the *The Parallel Curriculum* for an in-depth discussion).

Figure 1.1   The Components of Comprehensive Curriculum

Curriculum Component	Definition	Exemplary Characteristics
Content (standards)	Content is what we want students to know, understand, and do as a result of our curriculum and instruction. Standards are broad statements about what grade level students should know and be able to do.	Exemplary standards incorporate "big ideas," enduring understandings, and skills of a discipline. In addition, they provide clarity, power, and authenticity for teacher and students.
Assessments	Assessments are varied tools and techniques teachers use to determine the extent to which students have mastery of learning goals.	Well-designed assessments are diagnostic, aligned with the learning goals, and provide a high ceiling, as well as a low baseline, to ensure that all students' learning can be measured. They are used before, during, and after instruction. High-quality assessments inform instruction.
Introductory activities	An introduction sets the stage for a unit. Components may include (1) a focusing question, (2) a needs assessment to determine students' prior knowledge, interests, and learning preferences, (3) a teaser or "hook" to motivate students, (4) information about the relevance of the goals and unit expectations, (5) information about expectations for students, and (6) consideration of students' interests in or experiences that connect with the unit topic.	A high-quality introduction will include all six elements, as well as an advance organizer that provides students with information that they can use to help assess their acquisition of the unit's learning goals.
Teaching strategies	Teaching strategies are methods teachers use to introduce, explain, demonstrate, model, coach, guide, transfer, or assess in the classroom.	Beneficial teaching methods are closely aligned to learning goals, varied, promote student involvement, and provide support, feedback, and scaffolding for learners.
Learning activities	A unit's learning activities are those cognitive experiences that help students perceive, process, rehearse, store, and transfer knowledge, understanding, and skills.	Effective learning activities are aligned with the learning goals and efficiently foster cognitive engagement (i.e., analytic, critical, practical, and creative thinking) integrated with the learning goal.
Grouping strategies	Grouping strategies refer to varied approaches a teacher can use to arrange students for effective learning in the classroom.	Well-designed grouping strategies are aligned with the learning goals. Effective grouping strategies are varied and change frequently to accommodate students' interests, questions, learning preferences, prior knowledge, learning rate, and zone of proximal development. Group membership changes frequently.
Products	Products are performances or work samples created by students that provide evidence of student learning. Products can represent daily or short-term student learning or can provide longer-term, culminating evidence of student knowledge, understanding, and skill. High-quality products often double as assessment tools.	Powerful products are authentic, equitable, respectful, efficient, aligned to standards, and diagnostic.
Resources	Resources are materials that support learning during the teaching and learning activities.	Exemplary resources are varied in format and link closely to the learning goals, students' reading and comprehension levels, and learning preferences.

Curriculum Component	Definition	Exemplary Characteristics
Extension activities	Extension activities are preplanned or serendipitous experiences that emerge from learning goals and students' interests.	Powerful extension activities provide for student choice. They relate in some way to the content/standards, are open ended, authentic, and generate excitement for and investment in learning.
Modifications for learner need	Teachers can enhance learning by optimizing the match between the curriculum and students' unique learning needs. One kind of modification represented in the Parallel Curriculum Model is referred to as "Ascending Intellectual Demand."	Well-designed modification strategies are closely aligned with the learning goals and students' interests, questions, preferred learning modes, product preferences, prior knowledge, and/or learning rate.

Other issues that arise in developing solid curricula are the sequencing of the content and the allocation of time for learning each major piece of knowledge within a given curriculum unit. The most difficult part of creating a curriculum unit isn't making one "dish," or writing one lesson; it's how we go about making sure that all of the dishes on the menu are sequenced appropriately as first, second, and third courses throughout the duration of the meal (or curriculum unit).

A curriculum plan—especially one based on PCM—is more than raw ingredients or a disjointed set of entrees, and it has as much to do with the quality and quantity of the curriculum components and providing a generous source of energy and vitality as it does with the proper timing and sequencing of the lessons. Although this principle—that a good curriculum unit depends on well-sequenced and high-quality content, plus curriculum components that focus on powerful content and convey a sense of magic and energy for the learner—is a long-standing rule in the field of education, knowing this makes it no easier to achieve. It is vital that all with a stake in successful educational outcomes find a way to support those teachers who are enterprising enough to take on the role of PCM curriculum writer.

SUPPORTING THE WORK OF CREATIVE PROFESSIONALS

When master chefs help colleagues create their own original entrees and meals, they do so by sharing their methods for applying the basic principles, strategies, and generalizations that govern the culinary arts. They do not simply share existing recipes. A recipe is of little use to people who want to craft their own creations. The Culinary Institute of America (CIA) is not the venue for a cook who wants to learn how to follow other people's recipes any more than a PCM curriculum writing institute is appropriate for an educator who is interested only in implementing a previously designed PCM curriculum unit. Instead, the CIA and the challenge of writing PCM curricula cater to the same type of professionals—those who want to engage in the messy, complex, and sometimes frustrating job of creating a worthy product from scratch, a product that is designed to meet the unique learning needs of a select group of students who work and learn in a distinctive school environment.

This issue—how to assist educators who want to design PCM curriculum units from scratch—has been an ongoing concern since the publication of *The Parallel Curriculum* in 2002. Educators who share the vision of curriculum portrayed in the original book are usually interested in doing more than discussing the merits of the model or using someone else's PCM unit. Many are ready to begin the process of revising or creating new curricula that address one or more of the goals within the PCM.

Yet even these brave souls need a little help and support to create an outstanding PCM unit. They need access to the basic processes, strategies, and generalizations that govern the writing of Parallel Curriculum units, and they need the opportunity to collaborate with others during the difficult design and revision process. Our initial work with numerous educators who were interested in writing PCM curricula suggests that the use of specially designed protocols, prompts, and templates supports the design process and increases the likelihood that an exemplary curriculum unit will be developed.

Over the last year, the editors of this book have had the privilege of working with more than three dozen educators, some of whom were part of a federal grant project, to create, implement, and test more than 24 different PCM units in social studies and science. Our collaboration with the professionals in this cadre provided an ideal opportunity to identify and generalize a common structure, or protocol, that appears to describe the development of quality PCM curricula.

Like protocols designed by researchers and medical and emergency personnel, the PCM protocols I present here resulted from the careful observation, description, and synthesis of the work of varied professionals in order to discover and share the "secrets" of their curriculum writing expertise.

THE PARALLEL CURRICULUM MODEL PROTOCOLS

Step 1: Identifying the Content to Be Learned

As discussed earlier, the content educators want students to acquire is the most important consideration in designing a PCM unit. The content thus determines which parallel is emphasized and which, if any, of the other parallels may also be incorporated into the unit.

To select and prioritize the content for a PCM unit, educators might consult content reference books, state and national standards, or local content specialists. They might consider the related content that is taught (or not taught) in earlier or later grades or review the knowledge that is addressed in their textbooks. While all of these considerations are important, they are most likely to lead the curriculum writer toward only one parallel—the Core. If the grade level, program, or district team is interested in investigating the content possibilities that lie within the Connections, Practice, or Identity parallels, they need to consider other kinds of knowledge as well.

We found that the authors in our cadre often considered the multiple facets of their *own* existing understandings about the unit topic *before* they consulted reference books. In doing so, they were able to concentrate on the enduring, relevant, and powerful knowledge about the topic that they had retained throughout their school careers and well into their adult lives. This reflection process also allowed them to avoid the temptation of writing a curriculum unit that was simply a reiteration of what was already available to educators and, instead, create a unit that addressed the powerful knowledge related to the Core, Connections, Practice, and Identity parallels.

We experienced considerable success in helping authors who were not a part of our original cadre reach these alternative perspectives with the use of a paired or small-group activity we later named "The Most Important Things About X." We shared the popular children's picture book *The Important Book*, by Margaret Wise Brown (1990), and asked participants to assume that students who participate in the typical curriculum unit probably remember only a small fraction of the information and knowledge to which they are exposed. We invited the curriculum writers to consider what content students could, should, or would learn in their unit if they concentrated only on the most important aspects of that topic or subject: content that was powerful (had strong explanatory ability) and lasting (had relevance throughout one's life), or knowledge that had personal relevance or supported the development of personal mastery and expertise.

To activate the group members' most important prior knowledge about the subject matter or topic for the new, yet-to-be-written PCM unit, we asked them to work with a partner or in a small group and respond, in turn, to this prompt:

> What are the *most important things* you already know, think you know, wish you knew, or wish other people knew about your unit topic? Please take a minute to think alone and jot down a short list. Then, taking turns with your partner(s), state an item on your list in a complete sentence and listen as other group members do the same. Repeat this pattern until all items have been shared.

This activity requires between 10 and 30 minutes, depending on the size of the small group, and it is helpful if someone keeps a record of the list on notepads or charts for future use. The activity supports the development of a common vision with regard to the unit content and can yield interesting results. One group, working on a math unit about multidigit division, developed the following list:

1. Multiple-digit division can be really confusing unless you have a simple system to keep track of your thinking.

2. There is more than one way to do long division.

3. These days, a lot of people use calculators to perform long division.

4. Division is just the opposite of multiplication. If you can multiply, you can divide.

5. There are mental math strategies you can use to make long division easier.

6. A lot of people get really frustrated and angry when they have to do multiple-digit division. They probably wouldn't be so frustrated if they thought they could get better at it by using just a few new strategies.

7. Unless you estimate the answer first, you might end up with an answer that seems right but is really way off track!

8. To really understand multiple-digit division, you have to understand place value.

9. Most division problems in the real world require the use of multiple-digit division.

10. There are a lot of math problems in the world that require multidigit division.

11. If you can divide by one-digit numbers, you can divide by multiple digits.

12. Dividing is about putting a large number into small groups that all add up to the same large number.

13. Some of the tricks for performing multidigit division were invented by people in other cultures a long time ago or by people in ancient civilizations.

Consider this list from the perspective of the four curriculum parallels. Does this list, developed in less than 15 minutes, contain opportunities for students to explore Core knowledge about multidigit division? What about Connections to other time periods, cultures, or topics? Do you see any possibilities for teaching real-world strategies or Practices, or for addressing the way a student's Identity may influence how he or she learns the discipline of mathematics?

Of course it may be that all of these parallels cannot be included in one brief unit, and we will certainly need to consider state and national standards at some point in the decision-making process. However, this opening exercise is still powerful because it provides an opportunity for authors to view the topic from multiple perspectives and consider the inclusion of more than one parallel in their unit.

At this point in the process, there appears to be no need to make a definitive decision about which content will become the focus of the unit. Our goal in Step 1 is merely to identify powerful possibilities from our own and others' perspectives. For this reason, we might consider asking some group members to take on the role of students, while others may respond as teachers or still others as practicing professionals in the same or different fields of study. Asking one member of the group to serve as a timekeeper, another to act as a "shepherd" that keeps the group from drifting into tangents, and a third to act as a recorder of the ideas also seems to help the process.

Step 2: Telling a Story About the Content: Creating a Beginning, a Middle, and an End

A review of existing textbooks and curriculum guides frequently reveals a sad fact. The information students are supposed to learn and the activities they pursue often appear disconnected, or worse, superficial. To avoid this problem, most of the authors spent considerable time making decisions about the main ideas they wanted to include in the unit and the order in which they wanted to introduce and have students examine these ideas. In other words, the second step for most of the PCM unit writers was to take the relevant ideas they had identified in Step 1, write them as complete sentences, and sequence them so that they created a unit storyline with a logical beginning, middle, and end.

Although this "storyboard" was sometimes revised as the lesson plans were actually written or implemented, the early focus on ideas, instead of facts, and the related sequencing provided a much needed structure for linking the main ideas in a rational order. In the end, most authors were confident that this step in the decision-making process would result in greatly increased student understanding.

This sequencing step can be facilitated for writing teams simply by asking them to spend 20 minutes working alone with their ideas from the first step and a small pile of sticky notes. We found that having participants write each main idea for their unit as a complete sentence, using only one sticky note for each main idea, brings added clarity to this step. Tacking these notes to a wall—in sequential order—allows others in the group to "follow the logic" of another author's storyboard in order to provide feedback, ask clarifying questions, or share another perspective or possibility.

An example of this process might propose that the preceding sequence of content ideas for the multidigit division unit be ordered differently, such as the following:

1. There are a lot of math problems in the world that require multidigit division.

2. Dividing is about putting a large number into small groups that all add up to the same thing.

3. Division is just the opposite of multiplication. If you can multiply, you can divide.

4. If you can divide by one-digit numbers, you can divide by multiple digits.

5. To really understand multiple-digit division, you have to understand place value.

6. Multiple-digit division can be really confusing unless you have a simple system to keep track of your thinking.

7. A lot of people get really frustrated and angry when they have to do multiple-digit division. They probably wouldn't be so frustrated if they thought they could get better at it by using just a few simple strategies.

8. There is more than one way to do multidigit division.

9. There are mental math strategies you can use to make long division easier.

10. Unless you estimate the answer first, you might end up with an answer that seems right but is really way off track!

11. Most division problems in the real world require the use of multiple-digit division.

12. These days, a lot of people use calculators to perform multidigit division.

13. Some of the strategies for performing multidigit division were invented by people in different cultures or a long time ago by people in ancient civilizations.

Again, the opportunities to explore Core, Connections, Practice, and Identity content are apparent, but the statements have been rearranged and sequenced to promote introductory experiences, transitions, and the development of a more comprehensive scheme of understanding. This reordered sequence also provides the structure necessary to develop aligned and constructivist teaching and learning activities during the upcoming steps in the decision-making process.

Of course, there is more than one set of main ideas that an author might want to include in a curriculum unit about multidigit division, and there is more than one way to sequence this content. The important thing to consider is whether or not the ideas and the sequence include the most fundamental aspects of a topic (usually addressed in standards statements) and whether the ideas are presented in a logical order that supports student understanding and application. It is at this point that many of the authors turned to reference books and standards statements to ensure the inclusion of powerful ideas that they may have overlooked during the brainstorming process accomplished in Step 1.

Step 3: Categorizing the Knowledge and Determining Major and Minor Parallels

The third step used during the decision-making process involved the categorization of the content on their sequenced list (as developed in Step 2) to determine areas of emphasis and those of minor importance. To help facilitate this process, the cadre authors reviewed the six categories of knowledge (see Figure 1.2) discussed in *The Parallel Curriculum* in Chapter 3 and Figure 3.3 on p. 49. With these categories in mind, we prepared a content mapping chart (Figure 1.3, p. 18). When mapping the content using this chart, cadre authors listed the main ideas for their unit in the far left column, in sequence. They then "teased out" the related content students were to learn according to the column headings to the right. Using this approach, authors made sure that each row of their content chart contained a comprehensive description of the main ideas and the supporting knowledge that would be taught during each phase of the curriculum unit.

This content chart became a convenient way to trace the "flow" of a unit, and it also served as an alignment reminder during the development of the teaching and learning activities within the unit. Its third purpose was to facilitate communication among authors who, although working on different units, supported each other with ideas and feedback.

Perhaps the most powerful purpose of the content chart was to help us identify the natural opportunities in a given unit to address more than one curriculum parallel (see Figure 1.3, Column 2). We discovered that the articulation of the unit's

Figure 1.2   Structure of Knowledge Categories

Knowledge Category	Definition and Examples
Fact	A specific detail; verifiable information or data *Example: The capital of New York is Albany.*
Concept	A class of things; a category with common elements *Examples: capital, city, nation.*
Principle	A fundamental truth, law, rule, or doctrine that explains the relationship between two or more concepts *Example: Capital cities are often located along major transportation routes. Social, economic, political, and geographic factors influence the location of a capital city.*
Skill	A proficiency, an ability, or a technique; a strategy, a method, or a tool *Example: Locate capital cities using longitude and latitude. Use a map key to identify the symbol for capitals.*
Attitude Problem solving, transfer, and application	A belief, disposition, appreciation, or value *Example: Develop an appreciation for the cultural heritage of capital cities.* The ability to use knowledge to address a goal that may not be immediately understandable *Fxample; Examination of issues that might arise when a capital needs to be relocated.*

main ideas and related content, without the jargon and overemphasis on the "verb" that typically accompanies a behavioral objective, made it easier to discern opportunities to incorporate the various parallels. If, for example, we discovered that the vast majority of main ideas stressed the facts, concepts, principles, and generalizations that were central to a discipline, we knew that we had identified content related to the Core parallel. On the other hand, if we found we had chosen to concentrate on the skills, tools, techniques, and applications used by practicing professionals, we knew we were going to emphasize the Practice parallel. In a similar way, if the content chart contained numerous references to perceptions, attitudes, values, proclivities, beliefs, or mindsets, we knew that the unit would focus heavily on the Identity parallel. If we noticed that many of the themes, principles, or generalizations lent themselves to numerous topics or to other disciplines, time periods, events, or cultures, we could foresee a unit that emphasized the Connections parallel. If, however, the content chart addressed varied kinds of knowledge, we could anticipate a unit that might address all four of the parallels.

Step 4: **Name That Tune—Locating the Focal Points**

At this point in the planning process, several of us thought we were ready to begin writing the lesson plans that would make up the unit. We assumed that if we followed the sequence outlined in the content chart in Step 3, the ideas for the introductory, teaching, learning, and assessment activities would naturally follow. Nothing could have been farther from the truth.

We soon discovered that a main idea followed by supporting details (as delineated in one row of the content chart) do not a lesson plan make. Ideas for activities did not spring to mind merely by reading the appropriate row on the content chart. For several weeks, we struggled with the question of how to move from main ideas (depending on the unit, time allocation, and the age level of the students) to ideas for related lesson plans. Then it hit us. We needed to "chunk" the main ideas to identify three to five segments that could become the focal points for the teaching and learning activities of the unit.

This whole experience reminded us of that 1960s game show, *Name That Tune*. To win the contest, participants had to attend to a few carefully selected notes from a popular song in order to identify the entire tune. The fourth step in the design process was named accordingly.

During Step 4, the cadre authors considered the best way to epitomize or name the essence of one or more rows of their content chart. With some of the smaller units, however, this step merely required the identification of the one word or phrase that captured the essence of a particular row on the content chart. For example, the first main idea of the multidigit division unit as outlined in Figure 1.3 might be named "Finding Real-World Relevance" (see Figure 1.4).

On the other hand, we found that some of the rows of the content chart could be grouped together using one category, note, or label that characterized their similarities. For example, Main Ideas 2 to 5 of the multidigit division unit provide an example of an opportunity for "chunking." The content in this portion of the unit revolves around an understanding of the concepts and principles that define division. These ideas, collectively, could be renamed the "Concepts and Rules of Division" (see Figure 1.4).

The prompt we eventually developed asked the authors to review the content chart and to "circle the rows in the content chart (see Figure 1.3) that address a common factor and name that feature." It was fascinating to discover that playing the "Name That Tune" game with a unit became an easy way to identify the defining feature of each section of the unit's content knowledge (as shown in Figure 1.4).

Step 5: Selecting the Related Activities, Resources, Products, and Time Allocations

Once identified, the decisions made in Step 4 sparked an interesting discussion regarding the appropriateness of using inductive or deductive teaching methods with some or all of the unit segments and the option of beginning the unit with a bird's-eye view, a problem, or an appeal to the students' imagination. Of course, articulating the major focus for each segment of the unit (as in Figure 1.4) made it much easier to identify an appropriate approach to that segment and to design the related teaching and learning activities. First, however, we needed to remind ourselves of the time allocations for the unit as a whole and for each individual section of the unit. It is pointless to have a wonderful idea for a product, assessment, or activity if one can't allocate the time necessary to pursue these tasks. Once again, a chart provided the graphic organizer needed to communicate our decisions to others and to make the relationship between the content and the activities more conspicuous.

Figure 1.3 Mapping the Content of Our PCM Curriculum Units

Author _____ Unit Title/Content _____ Multidigit Division _____ Grade Level _____

Main Ideas	Time Allocation and Parallel	Principles and Generalizations	Concepts	Skills	Applications	Dispositions and Affective Objectives	Themes and Macroconcepts	Guiding Questions
1. There are a lot of math problems in the world that require multidigit division.								
2. Dividing is about putting a large number into small groups that all acd up to the same thing.								
3. Division is just the opposite of multiplication. If you can multiply, you can divide.								
4. If you can divide by one-digit numbers, you can divide by multiple digits.								
5. To really understand multiple-digit division, you have to understand place va ue.								
Etc.								

Figure 1.4   Mapping the Content, Activities, and Products of Our PCM Curriculum Units

Authors _____   Unit Title/Content _____   Grade Level _____   Time Allocation _____

Main Ideas (Chunked)	Time Allocation and Parallel	Principles and Generalizations	Concepts	Skills	Applications	Dispositions	Themes	Guiding Questions
Concepts and rules of division								
Finding real-world relevance								
Constructivist Teaching and Learning Activities	Assignments and Products		Resources	AID		Assessment		Extensions and Parallels

A blank chart, such as the content mapping chart depicted in Figure 1.4, was designed for this purpose.

At the top of this chart (in the first column) we listed the chunked main ideas identified in Steps 3 and 4. Below that, we considered and described the teaching and learning activities related to these chunked ideas that we had identified as most important for students to deeply understand (see Figure 1.4). Several of the writers also used charts from *The Parallel Curriculum* (Figures 3.7 to 3.10) to support their brainstorming and decision making with regard to teaching methods, learning activities, products, and resources. (These charts are reproduced here as Figures 1.5–1.8.)

Some of the authors preferred to begin this step in the process by concentrating on the products (see Figure 1.5) students would develop to demonstrate or apply

Figure 1.5   Real-World Products

Selected Products				
Advance organizer	Dance	Illustrated story	Pamphlet	Set design
Advertisement	Debate	Interview	Pantomime	Short story
Animation	Diagram	Invention	Paragraph	Silk screening
Annotated	Diary	Investment portfolio	Pattern	Simulation
bibliography	Dictionary		Photo essay	Skit
Argument	Diorama	Journal	Photo journal	Slide presentation
Assignment	Display		Picture dictionary	Small-scale model
Audiotape	Dramatic	Landscape design	Picture book	Social action plan
	monologue	Learning profile	Play	Song
Biography	Drawing	Lecture	Poem	Sonnet
Blueprint		Lesson	Portfolio	Stencil
Board game	Economic	Letter	Poster	Summary
Book jacket	forecast	Limerick	Pottery	Survey
Bulleted list	Editorial	Line drawing	PowerPoint	
Bulletin board	Elegy	List	presentation	Table
	Essay		Prediction	Terrarium
Calendar	Etching	Magazine article	Proposal	Textbook
Campaign	Experiment	Map	Protocol	Theory
Card game		Maze	Puppet	Think piece
Census	Fable	Memoir	Puppet show	Timeline
Ceramics	Fact file	Memorial		Topographical
Chamber music	Fairy tale	Montage	Questions	map
Character sketch	Family tree	Movie		TV documentary
Charcoal sketch	Festival	Museum exhibit	Radio show	TV newscast
Chart	Filmstrip	Musical composition	Reader response	
Choral reading			Reflection	Video
Chronology	Glossary	Newspaper	Reflective essay	Video game
Collage	Graph	Notes	Relief map	Vocabulary list
Collection	Graphic		Research report	
Comic strip	organizer	Observation log	Rubbing	Weather
Compact disc	Greeting card	Oil painting	Rule	instrument/log
Computer game	Haiku	Oral history		Web
Computer program	HyperCard®	Oral report	Science fiction story	Worksheet
Costume	stack	Outline	Scrapbook	Wrapping
Critique	Hypothesis	Overhead	Sculpture	paper design
		transparency		

Figure 1.6 Resources

Human	Nonhuman	
	Print	**Nonprint**
Content-area experts Older students Younger students Other students in the classroom Parents Other teachers of that grade Community members Teachers from other grade levels Other school personnel University personnel Business personnel Service organization personnel Retired senior citizens	Biographies Poems Plays Diaries Magazine articles Journals Web College textbooks Newspaper E-mails Nonfiction Fiction Historical fiction Literary analysis Manuals Maps Survey data Tables Charts Anthologies Textbooks Historical documents	Software Artifacts Tools Inventions Technology Antiques Posters Paintings Dioramas Models Realia Photographs Observations Experiments Situations Events Globes Videotapes Exhibits Costumes Designs Equipment Music

their understanding of the content in that section of the unit. Some began their work with a search for the resources (see Figure 1.6) that teachers and students might use to support learning and understanding. Others found it more useful to concentrate on the "verbs" that described the kinds of cognitive, research, and communication processes (see Figure 1.7) students would pursue to build their understanding of the content in the related section of the unit.

While all three approaches proved successful, as long as all aspects of the teaching and learning activities, resources, and products were strongly correlated to the content students were to acquire, the last approach proved to be our strongest assurance that the teaching and learning activities for students would be meaning-making, and not didactic, in nature. Tasks and activities that contained cognitive verbs (e.g., *observe, compare, classify, find* the cause, *search* for patterns, or *make* an analogy) ensured that students would use analytic thinking skills to develop their understandings. Other verbs (e.g., *examine* the author's credibility, *mount* a logical argument, *check* data for bias, *examine* sources for multiple perspectives, etc.) provided opportunities for students to use their critical thinking skills. The use of additional skills (e.g., decision making, problem solving, planning, creating, using the tools and methods of the adult professional, etc.) provided additional opportunities for

Figure 1.7   Cognitive Processes That Can Be Used to Design Learning Activities

Thinking Skill	Definition
Analytical thinking skills	**Various cognitive processes that deepen understanding of knowledge and skills**
Identifying characteristics	The ability to identify distinct, specific, and relevant details that characterize an object, an event, or a phenomenon
Recognizing attributes	The facility to discern and label general or common features of a set of objects
Making observations	The capability to perceive and select attributes of an object or experience
Discriminating between same and different	The ability to make fine discriminations among objects, ideas, or events
Comparing and contrasting	The facility to see similarities and differences among objects, events, and people
Categorizing	The ability to group objects or events according to some preconceived classification scheme
Classifying	The capability to extract relevant attributes of a group of objects, people, or phenomena that can be used to sort or organize the same
Ranking, prioritizing, and sequencing	The facility to place objects, events, or phenomena in hierarchical order according to some quantifiable value
Seeing relationships	The ability to see a connection or interaction between two or more objects or phenomena
Finding patterns	The ability to perceive and extract a repeating scheme in objects or phenomena
Determining cause and effect	The ability to see and extract the most powerful reasons or results for a given event or action
Predicting	The ability to see patterns, compare and contrast, identify relationships, determine cause and effect, and anticipate likely events in the future
Making analogies	The ability to identify a relationship between two familiar items or events and similar items and events in order to problem-solve or initiate creative productivity
Critical Thinking Skills	**Various thinking skills that are used to analyze and evaluate data and evidence in order to develop, judge the effectiveness of, or respond to an argument or position**
Inductive thinking	The ability to draw an inferential conclusion based on repeated observations that yield consistent but incomplete data
Deductive thinking	The ability to draw a logical conclusion from premises
Determining benefits and drawbacks	The ability to weight the advantages and disadvantages of a given idea or action
Determining reality and fantasy	The ability to distinguish between that which is fanciful and that which is true or actual
Identifying value statements	The ability to recognize statements that reflect appraisals of worth that cannot be supported through objective means
Identifying points of view	The ability to recognize that individuals and groups may have values and beliefs that influence their perspective on issues
Determining bias	The ability to ascertain information that is value laden
Identifying fact and opinion	The ability to distinguish between statements that can be proven and statements that reflect personal beliefs or judgments

(Continued)

Thinking Skill	Definition
Judging essential and incidental evidence	The ability to assess information and categorize it into useful and less useful categories
Identifying missing information	The ability to determine essential information that is not given or provided
Judging the accuracy of information	The ability to determine the precision of evidence that is presented
Judging the credibility of a source	The ability to assess whether the given information is believable, valid, and worthy to be considered
Recognizing assumptions	The ability to distinguish between information that is commonly accepted as true and information that is conjecture
Determining the strength of an argument	The ability to extract the reasons for an argument and evaluate the evidence as worthy
Identifying exaggeration	The ability to extract statements that magnify or overstate what is accepted as fact
Executive Processes	**Various cognitive skills that are involved in organizing, synthesizing, generalizing, or applying knowledge**
Summarizing	The ability to reduce a written or oral narrative to its essential components
Metacognition	The ability to consciously monitor, describe, and reflect upon one's thinking
Setting goals	The ability to set desirable outcomes in any situation
Formulating questions	The ability to develop relevant and precise queries related to any endeavor
Developing hypotheses	The ability to use prior observations to develop a possible explanation for an apparent relationship between two variables
Generalizing	The ability to use repeated, controlled, and accurate observations to develop a rule, principle, or formula that explains a number of situations
Problem solving	The ability to describe a problem, identify an ideal outcome, and to select and test possible strategies and solutions
Decision making	The ability to create and use appropriate criteria to select the best alternative in a given situation
Planning	The ability to develop a detailed and sequenced series of actions to achieve an end
Creative Thinking Skills	**Various cognitive skills that are involved in creative production**
Fluency	The ability to generate numerous ideas or alternatives to solve a problem that requires a novel solution
Flexibility	The ability to generate a wide variety of ideas to solve a problem that requires a novel solution
Originality	The ability to generate novel or unique alternatives to solve a problem that requires a novel solution
Elaboration	The ability to create a large number of details that explain a novel solution to a problem
Imagery	The ability to visualize a situation or object and to manipulate various alternatives for solving a problem without benefit of models, props, or physical objects

Thinking Skill	Definition
Using idea/product modification techniques	The ability to use techniques such as substituting, combining, adapting, modifying, making larger or smaller, putting to new uses, eliminating, reversing, or rearranging parts to make a more useful whole
Listing attributes	The ability to identify appropriate improvements to a process or product by systematically considering modifications to the original product's attributes
Brainstorming	The ability to work with others to withhold judgment while identifying varied, innovative, and numerous alternatives for solving a problem
Creative problem solving	The ability to identify, research, and plan to solve a problem that requires a novel, systematic solution

SOURCE: Burns, D. (1993). *A six-phase model for the explicit teaching of thinking skills.* Storrs, CT: University of Connecticut, National Research Center on the Gifted and Talented. Used with permission.

constructivist learning. We also discovered that the use of the chunked content chart (Figure 1.4) provided a thorough overview of the unit for teachers who would be using the unit but who were not part of the original writing cadre.

One caution that may be given to other PCM curriculum unit authors is to monitor this step in the design process carefully to target activities, resources, and products that are developmentally and culturally appropriate and that speak to the imagination, questions, and interests of the students. A unit can "fall flat on its face" at this juncture if authors cannot afford to spend enough time searching for creative and innovative tasks and assignments that pique students' curiosity, address personal relevance, and provide opportunities for awe and magic.

We also discovered that a few long-term activities and assignments, carefully structured and supported, could prove more effective than the use of several, short-term assignments and tasks. We found it was important to pay careful attention to a variety of teaching methods and strategies as well. Direct (deductive), Socratic (questioning), and indirect (inductive) instructions all have their place. (See the Continuum of Teaching Methods in Figure 1.8.) The teacher's role in explaining, demonstrating, describing, or applying new content is a critical phase that ensures learning will occur and new content will be retained and generalized.

Step 6: **Providing for Ascending Levels of Intellectual Demand**

At this point in the development process, several of the authors were ready to consider how they might go about adjusting the unit content and tasks to address the needs of students with varying levels of cognitive, academic, methodological, or affective expertise. We had several discussions about appropriate modifications for learner need and AID and concluded that our units must provide a means for teachers to identify differences in students' levels of expertise with regard to the unit's content by considering students' prior knowledge and opportunities to learn,

Figure 1.8   Continuum of Teaching Methods From Direct to Indirect

Direct Teaching	*Teaching Method*	*Definition and Benefits*
Direct teaching is a form of instruction in which the teacher provides explicit, clear, and "spelled-out" content, explanations, or skills to students.	Lecture	A deductive teaching strategy that consists of a carefully sequenced, illustrated oral presentation of content that is delivered to small and large groups of students; an oral presentation interspersed with opportunities for reflection, clarification, and sense making *Benefit: Effective, short-term acquisition of new content knowledge*
	Drill and recitation	A teaching strategy that helps students memorize and recall information with accuracy and speed *Benefit: Accuracy and speed in student's recall of factual-level information*
	Direct instruction	A method of teaching that consists of a teacher's systematic explanation of a new concept or skill followed by practice under a teacher's guidance *Benefit: Efficient and equitable knowledge acquisition*
	Strategy-based instruction	A method for teaching a cognitive strategy or procedure; the teacher explains and helps students acquire the strategy, models the strategy, and provides guided practice and feedback to students as they internalize the strategy *Benefits: Strategy acquisition; improved student efficiency and self-efficacy related to skill performance*
	Assisted instruction in the content areas	A range of methods to support or scaffold students' reading of nonfiction material in various content fields *Benefits: Strategy acquisition; improved student efficiency and self-efficacy related to skill performance*
	Graphic organizer	An instructional strategy that uses visual diagrams to help students understand content and thinking strategies *Benefit: Enhanced ability to organize, interpret, and understand contents and skills*
	Coaching	A teaching method in which teachers make criterion-referenced observations about a student's performance and provide immediate, specific feedback in order to improve the student's performance *Benefit: Proficiency with respect to physical or cognitive skills*
	Concept attainment	A method teachers use to help students understand the essential attributes of a category or concept; to achieve this goal, the teacher systematically leads students through a controlled discussion during which students compare and contrast characteristics of examples and nonexamples of the category or concept *Benefit: Acquisition of new categories, concepts, and macro concepts (e.g., vegetable, adjective, tragic hero, compromise)*
	Synectics	A teaching method in which teachers and students share or develop metaphors, similes, and/or analogies that build a bridge between students' prior knowledge or experience and new learning *Benefits: Acquisition of new knowledge, enhanced creative expression, and/or increased ability to generate creative solutions to problems*
	Demonstration/Modeling	A teaching method in which the teacher's actions and behaviors serve as an example for students who, in turn, are able to replicate the actions and behaviors in other contexts *Benefit: Acquisition of behaviors, skills, and dispositions*
	Socratic questioning	An instructional strategy in which the teacher poses a carefully constructed sequence of questions to students to help them improve their logical reasoning and critical thinking about their position on an issue; can be used as a technique to bridge students' current level of understanding with new knowledge that students need to acquire (Model tailored for older students in middle school and beyond) *Benefits: Acquisition of content related to social issues; enhanced ability to think issues through logically*

Teaching Method	Definition and Benefits
Visualization	An instructional strategy in which the teacher encourages the students to pretend and imagine; students do not speak. They can be asked to see themselves performing a skill or participating in an event at some time in the future, etc. *Benefits: Literal comprehension and transfer of procedures, reduced anxiety, increased likelihood of goal attainment*
Role playing	The involvement of students as participants and observers in a simulation of a real-world situation *Benefits: Growth and understanding as it relates to content; students' understanding of others' beliefs and values; problem-solving skills*
Cooperative learning	A teaching activity in which the teacher purposively uses small-group interaction to forward new learning and accomplish academic and social tasks *Benefits: Collaboration among students; deeper thinking and understanding; enhanced feelings of empathy for others*
Jurisprudence	A teaching strategy in which teachers provide students with the opportunity to collaborate in order to develop cases and persuasive arguments on all sides of an issue, a controversy, or a decision *Benefits: Critical thinking, analysis, evaluation, synthesis, oratory, and persuasive writing*
Simulation	An inductive teaching method in which students assume roles of people engaged in complex, real-life situations *Benefit: Increased likelihood that concepts and principles induced from the simulation will be transferred and applied to the real world*
Inquiry-based instruction	An inductive teaching strategy in which the teacher poses a task, problem, or intriguing situation, while students explore the situation across small changes in the data set and generate insights about the problem and/or solutions *Benefits: Increased self-awareness; awareness of different points of view; enhanced curiosity; increased understanding of concepts and principles; enhanced ability to solve problems*
Problem solving and problem-based learning	An inductive teaching method in which the teacher presents an ill-structured, novel, and complex problem for students to investigate and solve collaboratively with teacher guidance and coaching *Benefits: Acquisition of new knowledge, concepts, and principles; enhanced problem-solving ability*
Shadowing experiences	A teaching strategy employed by a teacher in which a student or a small group of students receives short-term exposure to selected fields or disciplines. A teacher may involve a student for several hours or several days *Benefits: Increased ability to use the tools and methodology of the discipline; increased understanding of the life of the practicing professional; a deepening awareness about the fit between a learner's profile and the targeted field or discipline*
Mentorship	A teaching method in which a student spends a period of time collaborating with an expert in the field in order to learn the content, methodology, and day-to-day activities of the practicing professional *Benefits: Enhanced content area knowledge; increased ability to use the tools and methodology of the discipline; increased understanding of the life of the practicing professional; a deepening awareness about the fit between a learner's profile and the targeted field or discipline*
Independent study	An instructional strategy in which the teacher encourages individuals or small groups of students to explore self-selected areas of study *Benefits: Enhanced motivation, content area knowledge, and methodological skills*

Indirect Teaching

A form of teaching in which the student takes an active role in constructing the content, knowledge, or skills to be acquired.

cognitive levels, learning rates, communication, reading, research skills, and/or their intrinsic motivation. This information would then be used to identify content, resources, and products and to create tasks that would challenge learners with advanced knowledge as well as all other learners who are at varying points of growth toward expertise.

We created a blank chart based on Figure 1.9 and used it to develop a profile of learners with different stages of development or proficiency. We relied heavily on our knowledge of the characteristics and behaviors of novice and advanced learners at a specific age level and called on the special education, English as a Second Language (ESL), and gifted education specialists in our cadre to help us determine whether our descriptors were valid. The descriptors themselves (e.g., from *novice* to *expert*) were not as important as the fact that teachers took time to delineate a progression of expertise. This mechanism for identifying students' current proficiency significantly helped teachers move them ahead in competency.

We soon found that describing AID was easier if we considered more than one factor in a learner's profile. We also discovered that the profiles we created were much more specific and useful than the data we had received from the typical achievement or cognitive abilities test.

When the profile was complete, we worked in pairs or in small groups to consider ways to escalate the content, resources, tasks, or products for students who were already proficient or demonstrated expertise. When appropriate, several of the ideas for AID were later listed in the corresponding sections of the lesson plans, as subsequently described in Step 10. Figure 1.9 contains an example of such a profile and related AID suggestions for a kindergarten unit on American history. Again, consultation with our education specialists helped us identify ideas that were challenging as well as enticing for our learners.

Once more, rereading sections of *The Parallel Curriculum* (see also Chapter 5 in that book) that addressed AID proved helpful to most of us as we considered how we might increase the challenge level of the unit for our most advanced learners. Talking and brainstorming with other writers were also extremely useful in getting us out of a rut and avoiding mundane, or "space filler" types of modification or enrichment activities.

Step 7: Considering Assessment as It Relates to Rubrics, Products, and Ascending Intellectual Development

As soon as we had completed the learner profile in Step 6 and designed several AID options, it became clear that we had already finished a lot of our "up front" work with regard to the unit's assessment. In other words, with just a little "tweaking," the profiles of novice, competent, proficient, and advanced learners on the learner profile might serve double duty as a rubric for measuring students' learning growth from the beginning to the end of the unit. All we had to do was add a comparable preassessment and postassessment.

One aspect of our work had to do with the traits for the assessment rubric. We often discovered that we had to add two to four additional traits to the rubric to address students' acquisition of related principles, generalizations, applications, connections, or attitudes. This kind of knowledge frequently had become a major

Figure 1.9   Profile of Learners at Different Stages of Expertise in This Subject Area and Grade Level

Subject Area/Topic: *American history*   **Grade Level**: *Kindergarten*

Describe the differences in students' stages of development with regard to this specific subject matter and grade level. Consider seven factors (prior knowledge, cognitive skills, learning rate, reading ability, communication skills, motivation, and research skills) across five stages of expertise (novice, basic, competent, proficient, and expert). Last, consider and describe AID activities for students who demonstrate proficiency or expertise.

Factors	Novice	Basic	Competent	Proficient	Expert
Prior knowledge	Can name things that are "old"	Can retell a family story about an event in the past	Can name 1–2 events, people, or places in American history	Can retell a historical story	Can relate several stories or anecdotes about American history
Cognitive skills	Can attend to instruction and recall and describe details about historical events	Can find similarities and differences in historical stories, events, artifacts, or places	Can make connections between historical events, people, stories, and their own lives	Sees cause or effect relationships among historical events and the present time	Makes inferences about historical events, people, or artifacts
Learning rate	Understands 2–3 historical concepts with 10 or fewer examples, explanations, or repetitions	Understands 2–3 historical concepts with 7 or fewer examples or explanations	Understands 3–4 historical concepts with 5 or fewer examples	Understands 3–4 historical concepts with 3 or fewer examples	Understands 5–7 historical concepts with 2 or fewer examples
Reading ability	Can follow the story line during a teacher read-aloud	Can retell content from a read-aloud	Can mimic read a class chart about a historical event	Can "read" a wordless picture book and remember the content	Can read a simple leveled book with contextual or phonetic cues
Written communication skills	Uses scribbles and invented spelling to write a caption	Uses sound-symbol skills and invented spelling to write a one-word caption	Uses sound-symbol skills and invented spelling to write a caption	Uses sound-symbol skills and invented spelling to write a short sentence	Uses sound-symbol skills and invented spelling to write a short paragraph
Research skills	Examines historical artifacts with prompting and support	Independently examines historical artifacts	Sustains self by skimming a book about history	Poses literal questions about historical events, people, or artifacts	Poses interpretive questions about historical events, people, or artifacts
Motivation	Attends to instruction for a brief time with prompting	Exhibits curiosity about history	Exhibits an intrinsic motivation for history	Exhibits enthusiasm for history	Exhibits a sustained interest in history

Describe how you might modify this lesson/unit/activity for students who demonstrate proficiency or expertise:

CONTENT

Provide books, videotapes, or stories about various eras, events, and people in American history. Concentrate on historical periods or events that are not familiar to even the most advanced students.

RESOURCES

Ask the school librarian to locate historical documentaries usually used with intermediate grade students. Make these available as AID opportunities during the unit.

TASKS

Display photographs of historical events, places, or artifacts and invite students to pose numerous historical questions about the topics. Ask students to answer their own questions using observation and inference.

PRODUCTS

Provide center activities that allow students to listen to historical stories on audiocassette and create written summaries and illustrations.

Create a display of historical picture books and museum artifacts. Invite students to examine the historical information and re-create the event or scene using improvisation, illustrations, or creative play materials.

content expectation for the unit but was not the type of content we could anticipate that even a few of the students would come to the unit already knowing.

Another challenging aspect of the assessment design process came when we realized that designing a preassessment that mirrored the postassessment was sometimes difficult to accomplish. If an author created a wonderful performance assessment that was seamlessly woven into the unit as a long-term application assignment and product, it didn't seem prudent to ask students to develop a similar product as a preassessment before instruction had even begun. In these situations, we found that students' journal entries or concept maps were more useful as preassessment tools.

We also discovered that the proper assessment format was strongly correlated to the kind of knowledge that students were expected to learn and the curriculum parallel(s) they were to experience. A multiple-choice test makes little sense if a teacher is trying to measure the extent to which a unit featuring a Curriculum of Identity affected students' habits of mind or self-efficacy. Instead, journal entries and reflection seem more appropriate. In a similar vein, students who participate in a Practice parallel unit should be able to demonstrate skill proficiency or the ability to solve problems and transfer learned Core Curriculum content to a novel situation. In other words, the form of the assessment should fit the nature or function of the unit's parallel(s) and content goals.

All of the authors agreed on the importance of assessing students' learning over the length of the unit and comparing that growth with grade-level expectations or with students' learning in past years. Without that information, we would never be sure if the unit was reaching its goals.

Step 8: **Reality Check: Aligning Content With Time, Tasks, Products, and Parallel Possibilities**

Describing this next step as the "eighth" step is somewhat arbitrary. In truth, most of the authors visited this "step" at least two or three times during the planning, decision-making, and development phases of their curriculum writing.

The best descriptor for this part of the protocol is "reality check." The purpose at this juncture is to verify that the content for the unit is well aligned with the activities students will pursue, the resources they use, the products they create, the parallels they explore, and the time allocated for their learning journey. This step is crucial to the development process in that it keeps us from getting lost and it keeps us honest.

Let's face it. Good ideas and time have a way of sneaking up on us, and if authors aren't careful, they can pack so many ideas and tasks into a unit that they are impossible to accomplish with any degree of integrity. Worse yet, the activities that seemed so interesting and necessary either end up overwhelming the content in the unit or leading students on a wild goose chase. And when students don't have time to pause and reflect on the purpose for the activities or when they can no longer find the big ideas, we have defeated our whole purpose for having the activities in the first place.

Step 8 is crucial for avoiding these problems, but this step can rarely be accomplished alone. We need the harsh eyes of a "critical" friend who meticulously analyzes each row in our content chart and each task in our lesson plans to make sure they make sense and need to be there. A colleague who provides only "warm" feedback is of little use to an author at this stage of the writing process. To succeed, an author has to find colleagues who are willing to be polite, but ruthless in their use of analytic questions that help us ferret out the illogic in some of our lesson sequences or the irrelevance of some of our products and tasks.

As painful as it may be, this "vetting" process assures us that our final draft will be well aligned, logically sequenced, and appropriated paced. This step is rarely achieved in less than three hours, and those three hours can seem like the longest and most agonizing of your life!

Step 9: **Creating the Introduction and the Debriefing for the Unit**

It may seem silly to include the design of the unit introduction within the ninth step of the development of a PCM unit, but it seemed to work for our cadre authors. Trying to do it any earlier created too many questions about the rest of the unit that couldn't be answered until all of the other lessons had been created. We also discovered that we needed to consider our learners' profiles so we could align our introduction accordingly.

As discussed on pages 52 and 53 of *The Parallel Curriculum* (Tomlinson et al., 2002), a unit's introduction can include as many as six different features:

- A focusing question derived from a standard or big idea of the unit around which the unit will be centered
- An advance organizer that informs students of the content they will explore
- A preassessment to measure what students already know about that content
- A motivating activity, or "hook," that intrigues students or excites them about the activities they will be pursuing
- A real-world application that demonstrates the relevance of the unit and its content
- An opportunity for students to share what they already know, or would like to learn, about the unit topic

Rarely does a unit include all of these components; instead, the learners' profiles dictate which elements should be included to promote engagement, provide structure, or demonstrate relevance. A simple graphic, similar to the one in Figure 1.10, can be used as a "menu" to help authors decide which introductory options are viable and necessary for a given unit and a specific group of students.

Once a decision is made about appropriate introductory activities, creativity moves front and center. Again, the opportunity to work with other authors, even if they are creating different kinds of units for students in different grade levels, supports the development of intriguing introductions and exemplary units. As with every other step in the curriculum writing process, working with colleagues encourages analysis, reflection, revision, and inventiveness. It helps us tolerate the frustration that is an inevitable part of the design process and assures us of support and feedback when we need it most. Cooperation is vital to this work, if for no other reason than the fact that team learning is essential when educators try to build reality from a common vision.

Figure 1.10   Selecting Introductory Components

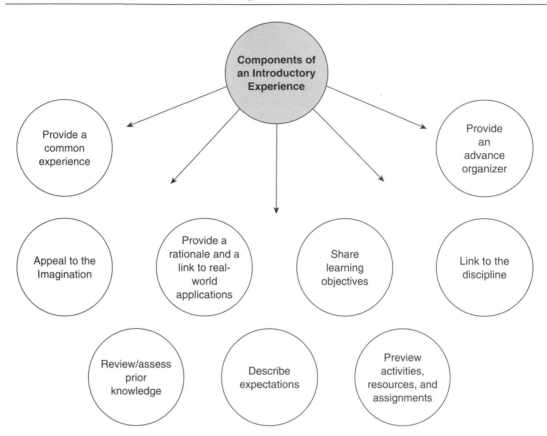

In a similar vein, the debriefing lesson at the culmination of a unit provides a unique opportunity to design a discussion or a journal writing assignment that encourages students to reflect on the new understandings they have developed. Like the debriefings that are conducted after an air force sortie or an armed forces mission, the purpose of a curriculum-based debriefing exercise is to help participants retell, remember, and retain key ideas and strategies and to support the drawing of conclusions that might have been overlooked in the flurry of the lesson. These conclusions are deemed useful for consideration and application in future learning and problem-solving situations.

Because the major purpose of a PCM-based curriculum unit is to support student learning across four different kinds of knowledge—Core, Connections, Practice, and Identity—it is logical that the debriefing reflections support those deep understandings. For example, at the conclusion of a second-grade science unit that studied the life cycle of a butterfly to teach life stages and the developmental sequence, we wanted students to realize that all organisms have life stages and that both genetics and the environment influence these stages. Although during the unit teachers had often mentioned the key Connections parallel principle, we remained unsure about the extent to which students had taken the time to reflect on that idea and come to the realization that when studying different organisms in the future they could predict that life stages were governed by both genetics and the environment. This uncertainty prompted our decision to include a reflection about the Connection parallel principle in our debriefing discussion. We designed a small set of open-ended questions for small group, paired, or written reflections that asked students to draw conclusions about the major ideas they had learned, to make an analogy between an idea they had learned and related topics, and to consider causes and effects, connections to self, and connections to the world at large.

One of the easiest ways to develop these questions is to base them on a small set of sentence stems that promotes such thinking and reflection. We used the chart in Figure 1.11 for that purpose.

Step 10: **Writing the Lesson Plans**

Bob Villa, the former host of the PBS series *This Old House,* is famous for the quote "Measure twice. Cut once." It is probably fair to say that the authors who wrote the 24 PCM units described in this essay measured nine times and cut once. That is to say, they spent 90 percent of their time planning and 10 percent of their time writing the actual lesson plans. Steps 1 through 9 are a testament to that fact. They are all about considering possibilities, viewing situations from multiple perspectives, weighing the disadvantages and the advantages, sequencing, arranging, categorizing, and analyzing. But at some point, even the most ardent planner has to start building the actual lesson plans.

When it came time to take the ideas, components, and sequence and turn them into a set of lesson plans, we realized that there was more than one way to do it. However, since communication, clarity, and efficiency were our chief concerns, we decided to opt for a common template that would make it easier for teachers who weren't part of the authors' cadre to read, understand, and implement the curriculum plan. We designed the template in Figure 1.12 for that purpose. It provides enough structure, detail, and description to foster understanding, but not enough to overwhelm the reader with too much verbiage or rigidity.

We anticipate that as teachers use their unit for the first time they will reflect on the surprises, successes, and difficulties in each plan. The notes they record in the margins can become discussion points at grade-level meetings and provide suggestions for improvement and revision. This "research lesson," as Japanese teachers refer to a prototype, will surely need to be revised and improved to suit the culture in different classrooms and the diversity among students in varying locales.

In a similar manner, we anticipate that the protocols, prompts, and graphic organizers described in this essay will be the topic of much discussion and experimentation over the coming years. The templates will invariably change and improve as more and more educators become PCM curriculum writers and reflect on the various ways they could make their experiences and expertise visible for others. The more we share our perspectives, insights, and strategies with others, the more knowledgeable and skillful we all become.

CONCLUSION

It is fascinating to watch the progression that occurs when an idea such as the PCM becomes a shared vision and that shared vision, in turn, becomes a source of creative

Figure 1.11   Topic Categories for Designing Debriefing Questions for Discussion or
Written Reflection

Reflection Category	Related Thinking Strategies	Sample Questions or Prompts to Scaffold the Reflection	Specific Questions or Prompts for This Unit
Core concepts, principles, or generalizations	• Inductive thinking • Observing • Finding relationships • Finding patterns • Classifying • Comparing and contrasting • Determining cause and effect • Prioritizing • Making predictions • Making generalizations	• What new terms have you learned in this unit? • What new rules and principles did you learn during this unit? • If you could only remember three ideas from this unit that we just studied, what would they be? • Why do you think these ideas are so important? • What is the most important thing you learned in this unit that an expert in this subject probably thinks is important too? • What ideas did you learn about this topic that you think will still be true and applicable for lots of other topics in this same subject area?	
Intra- or interdisciplinary connections	• Deductive thinking • Observing • Finding characteristics • Comparing and contrasting • Finding relationships • Making analogies • Determining cause and effect • Making generalizations	• If I told you that there were "twins" or maybe "triplets" in this unit, what do you think they would be? • What ideas of principles did you study in one topic that you saw reappear when you studied other topics? • Why do you think you saw similar ideas, rules, and patterns across the different topics you studied in this unit? • What ideas, rules, or patterns from this unit might reappear when you study other topics?	
Practice parallel skills, strategies, or applications	• Problem solving • Planning • Decision making • Making analogies • Evaluating • Determining relevant information • Sequencing	• What was practical or useful about this unit? • What kinds of problems did you solve in this unit? • How did you act like a professional in this field? • What was the hardest kind of thinking you had to do in this unit? • What kind of knowledge did you have to use to do your work in this unit?	

Reflection Category	Related Thinking Strategies	Sample Questions or Prompts to Scaffold the Reflection	Specific Questions or Prompts for This Unit
Identify parallel interests, values, or, developing expertise	• Metacognition • Evaluating • Planning • Decision making • Judging facts versus opinions • Prioritizing • Determining assumptions • Making value judgments	• What do you know how to do now that you didn't know how to do before we started this curriculum unit? • What was the best part of this unit for you? • What have you learned about yourself that you didn't know before we began this curriculum unit? • How, if any, have your ideas about yourself or this topic changed as a result of participating in this unit? • What do you want to do next, or in the future, as a result of this curriculum unit?	

Figure 1.12 PCM Unit Template

Unit Title

Module Number

(one module for each main idea or set of main ideas)

Title of This Module

Time Allocation

Related Parallels/AID

Assumptions to guide the creation of these modules:

1. If there are sections in this template that are not applicable to a particular module, place N/A in the appropriate space.

2. Boldface any titles of blackline masters, lab sheets, or other materials that students will use.

I. Module Overview

• 100–200 words
• Paragraph format
• Written for the teacher-user
• Reader friendly
• Summary of the module
• Describes what students will learn and do
• Mentions AID and/or other parallel opportunities

II. Guiding Questions

• Listed as questions
• Bullets
• Closely related to the module's main ideas
• Closely aligned to the assessment instrument(s)
• Labeled, in parentheses, for Core, other parallels, and/or for AID

III. Content Goals

Representative Topic(s)

• Listed when appropriate

(Continued)

Universal Theme

- Listed as a complete sentence when appropriate

Principles and Generalizations

- Written as complete sentences in easy-to-understand language
- Use bullets
- Labeled (in parentheses) as review, area of emphasis, AID, or parallel other than Core

Concepts

- One word or a phrase (definitions added as needed)
- Use bullets
- Labeled as review, area of emphasis, AID, or parallel other than Core

Related Information

- Listed as appropriate
- Use bullets

Skills

- One word or a phrase
- Instructional or application oriented
- Include cognitive, research, communication, or methodological skills

Dispositions

- Written as a sentence
- Written as a character trait, behavior, self-efficacy goal, self-reflection goal, or values statement
- Few in number

Application Opportunities

- Written as a sentence
- List opportunities in the module for transfer of learned content to a novel situation
- Few in number

IV. Materials and Resources

- Bullets
- Items, quantity, and size
- Complete bibliographic entries as needed
- AID references as needed
- List student and teacher resources
- Include copies of blackline masters

V. Preparation Activities

- Describe any work the teacher must do before this module begins
- List format

VI. Introductory Activities (Time Allocation)

- Bullet or paragraph format
- 100–150 words
- Introductory experience should be able to be conducted in 3–20 minutes
- Explain the activities, advance organizers, discussions, discussion questions, class meetings, shared experiences, community resources, audio-visual resources, demonstrations, or read-alouds that will be part of this activity
- List the activities in chronological order
- Make sure the activities are motivating and that they provide a preview of the modules' learning objectives
- The introductory activities may include an informal preassessment activity

- The introductory activities should include an opportunity to connect to students' background knowledge and experiences
- Include AID questions or activities as appropriate
- Link introduction contents to Learner Profile

VII. Preassessment (Time Allocation)

- Optional for the module, but required for the unit as a whole
- Individual, small, or large group
- Formal or informal for each module
- Formal performance assessment for the entire unit
- Unit preassessment samples the unit's content knowledge and mirrors the postassessment
- Unit postassessment requires the application of sampled content to an authentic scenario
- Aligned to guiding questions

VIII. Teaching and Learning Activities

- Time allocations should also be listed by activity
- Complete sentences
- Numbered
- Each segment describes the teacher's and the students' activity and the knowledge to be gained
- Incorporate the grouping practices within the paragraph
- Use complete sentences
- Use the second person, *you* understood (command form: "Arrange students in groups of three to four students.")
- Describe both the teacher's and the students' roles
- Whenever possible, employ constructivist teaching and learning activities
- Minimize the amount of passive learning
- Be realistic about time estimates
- Reference related blackline masters or skill strategies
- Incorporate AID (as appropriate) suggestions (labeled as AID in parentheses) or an extension activity at the end of the module
- Incorporate opportunities for/descriptions of assignments and products
- May incorporate application activities
- May incorporate parallel activities or questions (labeled appropriately)

IX. Products and Assignments

- Bullets
- List format
- Include the title of the assignment
- Include directions for completing the assignment in the appropriate section of the teaching and learning activities
- List AID options (titled as such in parentheses)
- Include parallel options (listed as such in parentheses)

X. Extension Activities

- Independent activities for individuals or small groups
- Mandatory or optional
- AID for all students
- Could incorporate one or more parallels
- Homework, contracts, or centers
- Debriefing questions or prompts for reflection, discussion, or writing assignments
- Do not have to be lengthy or complex
- Materials must be listed under the "Materials and Resources" section, labeled as such
- This section could contain a list of possible extension activities
- List time estimates (in parentheses) for each suggested extension activity
- This section should be no more than one-half page in length

XI. Postassessment

- Optional for a given module but should be included in several modules
- Brief

(Continued)

- Contains a four-level holistic or trait rubric
- Closely aligned to the preassessment and the guiding question(s) for this module
- Varied format (observation, work sample, performance, conference, concept map, reflection, essay, etc.)
- Optional for the module, but required for the unit as a whole
- Individual, small, or large group
- Formal or informal for each module
- Formal performance assessment for the entire unit
- Unit assessment samples the unit's content knowledge and mirrors the preassessment
- Unit postassessment requires the application of sampled content to an authentic scenario
- Aligned to guiding questions

XII. Debriefing and Reflection Opportunities

- Opportunity to review and focus the module's content and activities
- Linked to the discipline
- 10–15 minute discussion, think-pair-share, or reflection format
- Could incorporate students' concept mapping, journal reflections, and connections to self or other parallels
- Emphasize the relationship between the module's content and activities and real-world applications
- Bullet format

tension, team learning, and planning. The lengthy and spirited conversations and debates about various aspects of the PCM—its philosophical underpinnings and its historical roots—are gradually making way for different discussions about professional development, curriculum writing, implementation, student assessment, and curriculum evaluation. The collegial nature of this venture continues, but the challenges are ever changing.

As participants in this journey, we are excited about the possibility of testing our newly developed PCM units with students from several different school districts over the coming years. We are just as interested in using our protocol and templates with new groups of authors who are curious about PCM and intrigued about being curriculum writers. Will the protocol be useful in "upscaling" PCM? Will the templates make it easier for others to write PCM curriculum, or is the process so unique and special to every individual or small group that the templates become straitjackets instead of a support system?

Time will tell, but one thing is certain. The path we are traveling is by no means the "rutted road" of curriculum that the Romans described in ancient times. PCM represents an evolutionary approach to curriculum development that envisions four unique and powerful formats for the following: expanding content expertise by exploring the structure of a discipline, helping students achieve a deeper understanding by investigating relationships and analogies, enticing them to learn and excel by seeing themselves reflected in the topics they are studying, and showing them how to use their knowledge by applying it to authentic concerns and bona fide applications. PCM is indeed a new path, in need of scouts and pioneers who are willing to prepare the road for all learners.

The Importance of the Focusing Questions in Each of the Curriculum Parallels

Jann H. Leppien

Early in my teaching career, I met a young man named Sam who possessed a great deal of mathematical expertise at a young age. He arrived at our school at the age of five and entered kindergarten ready to learn with great intensity and enthusiasm. Mrs. McDonald, his kindergarten teacher, was eager to work with Sam and to provide an educational setting that fostered his love of mathematics.

Mrs. McDonald's first encounter with Sam's level of expertise was when he revealed to her that he thought he should move to the state of Connecticut because he did not think he was worth very much money to the schools in Montana. He continued to tell her that even though this made him feel badly, he was comforted by the fact that the governor should probably leave with him and go to Connecticut, since the governor's salary would be higher in this state when compared to the salary he was receiving in Montana. When asked how he had acquired this information, he pointed to the education and government sections of the world almanac that he had brought to school and proceeded to inform Mrs. McDonald of all the wonderful uses of mathematics this text provided, including a ranking of the governors' salaries in each of the 50 states and the amount of money each school received per child as reported by each state.

Each and every day, Sam would use mathematical language to explain his observations. The mathematical content and skills that were of importance to most kindergarteners seemed more and more out of alignment with his mathematical knowledge and understanding. It was soon decided that we should pretest Sam to determine a starting point for his mathematical instruction, and I was given the opportunity to help determine his level of proficiency. I soon realized that Sam not only had great expertise in mathematical understanding but also had an unusual way of learning new concepts.

First and foremost, Sam enjoyed the testing situation. For him, the test was a game of mathematical reasoning and inquiry. He delighted in arriving at the correct responses, and he pursued ideas that were unfamiliar by asking a series of questions that he soon answered for himself. What was of particular interest to me was how he approached what he did not know. For example, I can remember, quite vividly, how excited he became when faced with a fraction problem in the third-grade curriculum. The question asked Sam to look at two circles, one that was divided into three parts and one that was divided into four parts (one representing 1/3 and the other representing 1/4). He was asked to name the fraction that was largest, one-third or one-fourth.

As he looked at these circles he asked, "What is this thing called? Everything has a name, Mrs. Leppien, so what do you call these things?"

I replied that these visual representations are called fractions.

He then asked me, "Is this like a pie that is cut into several pieces? If it is, then my mother certainly can't cut straight lines like they do in this picture. My guess is that the question they are asking is which of the pieces of pie would I prefer, either one-third or one-fourth?" As quickly as he asked the question, he announced, "But it would have been easier had they asked me to compare these pieces as twelfths or twenty-fourths, or something that they share in common."

Sam's line of questioning stemmed from his curiosity to know and also from his ability to see patterns and make connections between mathematical ideas. Once he understood the structure of anything—its purpose, examples, and importance to his life—he then questioned how to play out these ideas in various settings and under different conditions, similar to the way writers play with word choices in constructing sentences that express ideas. Sam would then move toward trying to see patterns or connections between concepts and ideas in order to state laws or what he referred to as "mathematical rules to live by." Sam considered himself to be a mathematician, and this became the lens through which he viewed the world.

I learned that the questions teachers ask are like the questions Sam posed to himself and others. They can provide rich invitations for developing student engagement and for promoting understanding of a discipline's structure, its connectivity to other disciplines or ideas, its modes of inquiry, and how it shapes or affects an individual's life. In the Parallel Curriculum Model (PCM), the focusing questions we have generated serve as a vehicle for selecting and organizing course content and for envisioning how the ten components in an effective curriculum can take shape as one designs a unit of study (see *The Parallel Curriculum,* Tomlinson et al., 2002).

THE NATURE OF A DISCIPLINE AND HOW IT RELATES TO THE FOCUSING QUESTIONS

The disciplines serve as points of entry for considering the deepest questions we have about the world. Disciplinarians often struggle for years in pursuit of their own answers to some essential question about life. As teachers, however, it is easy to forget that the topics we teach have value in helping students pursue these same types of questions about issues that concern us as human beings.

Knowing how to use the tools and to ask the questions that these disciplines use to probe the meaning behind phenomena can guide teachers as they assist young people in making sense of their own world. Teachers who shape good questions assist students in looking through the lenses of many disciplines, requiring their students to wrestle with the factors that influence a certain event or inviting students to struggle intellectually with the meaning behind the content presented in a unit of study. In other words, when teachers realize that the content making up required curricula originated as essential and topic-specific questions whose answers lead to deeper understanding within a subject area and across disciplines, they can be thoughtful in orchestrating a series of questions or designing a set of learning tasks that will invite students to wonder about the content. When engaged in thoughtful questions and tasks, students are also led to understand why this information is important to them, compare this knowledge with other ideas in other disciplines, learn how scholars study a particular field of study, and explore how these related ideas connect to the students' lives and experiences.

To keep the value of essential questions uppermost in our thinking when creating and teaching PCM units, we can use the focusing questions for each parallel of the PCM. These questions are purposeful in expanding the conceptual understanding of a topic or discipline. These questions help to focus and shape the content-level instruction within each of the parallels. Asking these questions serves not only to organize content but also to strengthen students' sense of their own authority over the content. Each set of questions has specific ways in which it encourages students to use their minds well as they wrestle with the content. Some questions lean toward content mastery, whereas others require students to apply this content in new settings. For example, the Core Curriculum questions ensure that students focus on facts, concepts, principles, and skills. The focusing questions in the other three parallels offer students a chance to (a) see the concepts, principles, and skills at work in other contexts (Curriculum of Connections), (b) understand how experts in a field do their work (Curriculum of Practice), and (c) extend their understanding of themselves by comparing their own skills, perspectives, and goals with those of experts in the disciplines and/or people studied through the disciplines (Curriculum of Identity). By actively carrying out assignments that use these questions, students draw upon the fundamental information, ideas, and methods of the discipline—but do so with different emphases, depending on the parallel or parallels that shape the curriculum. These questions can also be used to develop writing prompts, create student activities and products that will provide evidence of student understanding, and design independent studies or interest options for students to explore areas related to the unit of study.

EARLY IN THE CURRICULUM PLANNING PROCESS

In the Core Curriculum, the guiding questions become those that focus on the key ideas, facts, and skills that are essential to a discipline or field of study. These ideas, facts, and skills serve as foundational knowledge and must be determined prior to designing the learning experiences, which become the means through which students make sense of the ideas. It is through this conceptual lens that the content and questions behind given topics can be illuminated and explored. Teachers who focus on the conceptual lens early in the planning phase ensure that a selected topic can become more generative in nature, thus leading to more opportunities for students to explore these ideas in further depth using the other parallels. When this conceptual lens is identified, it provides a framework for deciding which dimensions are important to pursue and which relationships of facts and ideas students should grapple with critically, comparatively, and creatively.

For example, it is far easier to organize the content of the Lewis and Clark expedition, Westward expansion, and other such explorations under the conceptual lens of "explorations" than to first introduce the details of each specific event. Turning core ideas of exploration into questions naturally leads to having students consider the purposes of exploration, the characteristics of those who explore, the causes that gave rise to the exploration, and the possible effects these varied explorations had on other cultures and on individual lives. The questions that we have generated for the Core Curriculum help students probe the meaning behind these questions to ensure that students develop a framework of knowledge, understanding, and skills that prepare them for a journey toward expertise in a subject area or discipline. Once a teacher comes to understand these questions and how they vary among the parallels, they can serve as useful tools for other curricular planning.

USING THE CORE CURRICULUM'S PURPOSE, CHARACTERISTICS, AND QUESTIONS TO GUIDE CURRICULAR DECISIONS

Although the focusing questions serve to provide a particular focus for an instructional unit, educators have found it helpful to use these questions to address some of the central decisions that will be made when designing some of the key components of an effective curriculum. In the preliminary planning stages of a curriculum unit, a teacher can find it helpful simply to begin the process by being generative about these elements of design. Using the purpose, the characteristics, and the students' questions as prompts for thinking helps us to become explicit about what we want our units of instruction to accomplish. To begin this process, one may use the purpose, characteristics, and focusing questions of the Core Curriculum in Figure 2.1.

The template in Figure 2.2 represents how teachers can begin to use the purposes, characteristics, and focusing questions of the Core parallel to generate potential ideas that may become part of their instructional unit. The template includes sections for a teacher to record possible questions that could be explored by the students within the Core Curriculum; introductory activities that set the stage for learning about the unit of study; teaching and learning strategies and activities that make up the cognitive and affective experiences that help students perceive, process, and transfer knowledge, understandings, and skills; products, performances, or work samples that can be used to assess student learning; and other categories that facilitate the development of a comprehensive unit of study.

Figure 2.1   The Core Curriculum's Purpose, Characteristics, and Focusing Questions

---

Purpose of the Core Curriculum

The Core Curriculum is the starting point for conceiving all effective curricula. It is defined by the nature of a given discipline. The purpose of the Core Curriculum is to ensure that students develop a framework of knowledge, understandings, and skills that prepare them for a journey toward expertise in a subject area or discipline. National, state, and/or district learning goals for students should be reflected in the Core Curriculum.

Characteristics of the Core Curriculum

The Core Curriculum does the following:

- Stems from the key facts, concepts, principles, and skills essential to a discipline
- Reflects what experts in the discipline find most important
- Is coherent in its organization in order to help students build knowledge, understanding, and skills systematically and organize what they learn in ways that develop students' abilities to remember, make meaning, and use what they know in unfamiliar situations
- Is designed to cause students to use consistently high levels of critical and creative thinking as well as metacognition to grapple with ideas and problems
- Is taught in contexts that are authentic to the discipline and meaningful to students, and in ways that are mentally and affectively inviting to students
- Engages students in worthwhile production that uses understandings and skills central to the discipline to address problems, dilemmas, and issues also central to the discipline

Questions That Students Ask in the Core Curriculum

Students ask the following questions in the Core Curriculum:

- What does this information mean?
- Why does this information matter?
- How is the information organized to help people use it better?
- Why do these ideas make sense in my life?
- What are these ideas and skills for?
- How do these ideas and skills work?
- How can I use these ideas and skills?

The following paragraphs illustrate how to use the template in generating ideas for a curricular unit on poetry. To begin the planning for this unit, however, a teacher needs first to generate what students will know, understand, and be able to do as a result of their participation in this unit. For example, the content in the Core parallel might include the following:

Knowledge

The definition of fiction, poetry, style, points of view, plot, conflict, voice, narrative, imagery, character development, context clues, and temporal time

Concepts

Voice and identity

Understandings and Principles

- People develop an identity throughout their lives.
- Our identities matter to us.

- Our identities are shaped by intentional acts and chance occurrences.
- Writers explore the identities of characters to help readers explore their own identities.
- Writers' voices reveal much about their identities.
- Voice reflects culture, personality, time, and opinions of the writer.
- Voice is both influenced by and an influence on literary form.

Skills

- Use context clues for determining the meaning of text.
- Read and write many types of poetry.
- Describe the visual images created by language.
- Analyze and apply how word choice, speaker (voice), and imagery elicit a response from the reader.
- Compare and contrast plot and character development in poems, short stories, and longer fiction selections.
- Establish central idea, organization, elaboration, and unity.
- Apply understandings about voice and imagery to elicit reader response.
- Edit final copies for correct language use and mechanics.

Once the content and skills framework for the unit has been determined, a teacher can begin to use the template in Figure 2.2 to explore the purpose and focusing questions of the Core Curriculum in relation to other categories of curricular decision making. Likewise, after brainstorming ideas to fill the template, a teacher needs to ask him- or herself, "How does what I have generated fit the purpose and focusing questions of the Core Curriculum?" Without this internal audit, teachers may return to what they have always used in their standard poetry unit without careful reflection as to its purpose and intent.

Nevertheless, some curricular activities may need to undergo slight revisions to clarify the goals of the learning task or to specify the type of thinking and procedures that students will use to process the ideas presented in the unit. It is also possible that a teacher may find that previous lessons do not really accomplish the curricular goals set forth in the Core Curriculum and should be eliminated. *Seeking clarity in what we ask of students* is the goal in this planning process.

The teaching and learning activities, journal prompts, questions, and learning stations described in Figure 2.2 set the stage for deepening the meaning of this unit's ideas. By generating these curricular ideas, we help students ask and answer the following questions: What is so important about these ideas, and how does knowing this assist me as a learner? The answers to these questions provide the background for asking students to look at key information, concepts, principles, and skills across multiple contexts and leads to deeper understanding of the central ideas of the curriculum unit of study.

USING THE CURRICULUM OF CONNECTIONS' PURPOSE, CHARACTERISTICS, AND QUESTIONS TO GUIDE CURRICULAR DECISIONS

As teachers or curriculum writers move toward designing the curricular elements that will be included within a Curriculum of Connections lesson or unit, they are

Figure 2.2   A Template for Getting Started With the Core Curriculum

---

Pose Focusing Questions

Ask students to consider the following:

- What does it mean to have a personal identity?
- How are identities formed?
- What does personal identity reveal about someone?
- How do writers reveal their voice?
- How does the writer help us to understand that Jack's identity changed over time?

Consider Introductory Activities

- Read aloud several poems that have strong voice, and ask students to identify the writers' point of view or their identity. In this brief introduction, have students identify what the poems reveal to us as readers and what literary techniques each writer uses in creating this voice.
- Place samples of poetry around the room in different locations. Have students rotate through the collection of poetry and select those poems that best represent their own voice or those that are like themselves in character, belief, or point of view. Upon returning with their selections, students will tell the class why they have identified with a poem. They may also develop a list of traits and elements about a writer that his or her writing reveals.
- Have students read *Love That Dog*, by Sharon Creech, in small groups. Have students identify how the writer revealed that the main character (Jack) grew in his ability to reveal his identity and voice. Ask how his poetry reflected his identity and whether his identity changed over the course of the year.

Generate or Add Activities to Current Curriculum

Ask students to do one or more of the following:

- Select two poems represented in *Love That Dog* plus one other of your choice. First, list traits or elements about each writer that his or her voice suggests to you. Use sticky notes to locate and record lines from the poems that guide your conclusion as well as why you drew those conclusions.
- Next, use your conclusions to guide your writing of a piece of poetry or prose that reveals the writer's voice and identity as you see it. Again, explain your thinking. You may work alone or with one partner to complete this task.
- Examine a topic or issue you believe that author would write about and consider how his or her identity would shape his or her expression. Combine prose and poetry to reveal what it is like to work with that writer's process, voice, and identity.

Develop Journal Prompts

Ask students to do the following:

- Explain the importance of being able to identify a writer's voice as you read.
- Respond to the following questions: What are the characteristics of a strong voice? How does one acquire a strong voice in writing?
- Consider the story of the Ugly Duckling. How did the author reveal his voice and identity to you throughout the story?
- Consider a time when your voice was strong, when what you said reflected what you believed or addressed a concern that you had. Explain the situation and then recall how strong your voice was. How did what you believe shape your voice?
- Consider a time when your voice was silent. Identify the causes for this silence and explain how this might influence your writing and speaking.

Create Interest/Independent Options

Post the following activities for students to pursue at learning stations, located at the back of the classroom:

Learning Station #1. Poetry Speaks

Select four to six poems from Paul Fleishman's book *Joyful Noise: Poems for Two Voices,* and place them in a folder for the students to use. Have students work together to select one poem they would like to perform with a partner. Together the students must determine how they will express the voices within the poem. Students must also explain their interpretation of the writer's voice and identity and how this has shaped their performance.

Try a Different Teaching Strategy

As I think about the Core Curriculum parallel, I am going to have students identify what poetic expression reveals to us about the writer. This will require that I change the way that I have introduced poetry to my students in the past. I will now select a variety of poems from which students can identify the traits or elements about a writer that his or her writing reveals. I think that I will use data-retrieval charts and provide students with sticky notes to capture what they find out in their investigations. Through engaging in analysis tasks, students will look for examples that provide evidence that a writer's voice reveals much about his or her identity, help students to know what is of importance to a writer, and in some cases help students to

(Continued)

Learning Station #2. Poetry Helps Us See

Ask students to turn on a tape recorder and listen to three to four poems that you have recorded. These poems should create vivid pictures for the listeners as you read each selection. Instruct the students to close their eyes and visualize the images, words, or messages created as they listen to these poems. Ask students to draw or paint what they saw in their minds when the poem was read to them aloud. These paintings should be posted with student explanations revealing why they created this particular image and how it relates to the images they "saw" when the poem was read to them.

Learning Station #3. Poetry Helps Us Feel

Place several types of poetry at this station. Ask students to choose a poem that they think really connects to their lives—that makes them feel something. Discuss with students how poetry comes from things that are deeply felt (love, anger, conflict, beauty, confusion, etc.) and why poetic expression is one form through which writers reveal what is important to them. Ask students to discuss the feelings generated by the poems they chose and share those feelings. In their reading notebooks, students may respond to the ideas that poetry can be "felt" and that the things important to them, as writers, can affect the writing of their own poetry.

Have students take one poem as a model to write an original poem that reflects something they feel deeply about. After they have written their poem, they should have other people read it and try to identify characteristics of the writer's voice.

Upgrade Products/Assessments

Using several of the elements listed under the Characteristics of the Core Curriculum, listed in Figure 2.1, I have decided to upgrade my products to be more reflective and responsive to the suggestions. Some examples follow:

- Stems from the key facts, concepts, principles, and skills essential to a discipline. (As students read poetry they will be asked to interpret voice and to identify the writer's identity through multiple points of entry. Students will be asked to locate or create visual illustrations of the writer's voice, design choral performances that help to reveal the writer's voice, and formulate personal examples of what the writer is trying to say to us as readers.)
- Reflects what experts in the discipline find most important. (I will ask students to explain the importance of the writer's work in helping us to understand issues that he or she feels deeply about. I will ask students to record what they believe is most important in the writer's message and how the voice helps us to understand something more clearly, or to agree or disagree with what a writer is expressing and to compare their own voices with that of the writer.)

realize that their own voices about issues, concerns, and so on can be expressed through this literary form as well. They will also come to understand that writers commonly write about things that are universal to all of us, thereby allowing us to identify with a writer's experiences about life. To have students arrive at these understandings, I must use both inductive and deductive strategies to prompt their thinking.

Evaluate Current Curriculum

My district curricular guide provides examples of poetry of famous poets, using different formats to express the poets' ideas. The curricular guide discusses a writer's use of poetry to express his or her ideas but does not place the focus on voice and identity. I can use parts of my current curriculum materials and resources as examples for students to read, but those activities do not promote what I want to have students understand, know, and be able to do.

To update and expand my curricular unit, I can use the Internet to locate resources that may be more interesting to the students. For example, I found a site, provided by the Library of Congress, that teaches the students how to read a poem (www.loc.gov/poetry/180/p180-howtoread.html). On this site, students can listen to Poet Laureate Billy Collins talk about how to read a poem. This tool can be used to strengthen students' understanding that the way a poem is read affects the interpretation of the message. This also reminds me to invite local poets into my classroom to speak about how their writing reflects their voice and why they chose this literary form to express their voice.

- Is coherent when its organization helps students systematically build knowledge, understanding, and skills and organize what they learn in ways that develop students' abilities to remember, make meaning, and use what they know in unfamiliar situations. (By placing the focus of this unit on voice and identity, I help students establish the purpose of writing. If students understand that writing is a voice that expresses and reveals identity through characterization, this can greatly help them better organize all types of writing, not only poetry. This concept is foundational to all writing and can be revisited throughout the year as the class moves through various genres. It also helps students to realize that part of the job of understanding expression is also to understand the voices behind the expression and how these voices reflect human life.)
- Is designed so that students use consistently high levels of critical and creative thinking as well as metacognition to grapple with ideas and problems. (Students will be asked to analyze and interpret voice and to apply voice to their own writing to elicit reader response. Students will be asked to locate examples and provide explanations of where a writer reveals his or her voice.)
- Is taught in contexts that are authentic to the discipline and meaningful to students, in ways that are mentally and affectively inviting to students. (Students are asked to wonder about the purpose of voice and identity in writing. These are natural inquiries that pique the curiosity of all minds despite one's age. Each of us wants a voice; we have each experienced times when our voice was silent or when we were uncertain about our voice, as well as times when our identity was revealed through the actions we took or the writings we created.)
- Engages students in worthwhile production that uses understandings and skills central to the discipline to address problems, dilemmas, and issues also central to the discipline. (Readers' response and text interpretation are vitally important to the discipline and allow a reader to come to understand what is being expressed and how it is expressed in a variety of literary forms. I have formulated my list of knowledge, understandings, and skills from understanding that writers use their voice to reveal their identity, express it in a variety of ways, and use certain skills to express it best. In my thinking about student activities, journal prompts, learning stations, and so forth, I have generated products that focus on these core ideas. In this section of my unit, students will grapple with these ideas through applying the following skills: (1) using context clues to determine meaning, (2) reading and writing a variety of poetry, (3) describing the visual images created by language, and (4) applying understandings about voice to elicit reader response.)

I will also need to locate poetry that reflects the diverse population in which we live. Our text includes some poets and writers, but not enough to have the students realize that all writers express their identities and experiences through the written word and that the experiences of all writers from diverse cultures must be read and analyzed to understand the universality of the expressions.

In some cases, I will organize my reading selections by theme so students can begin to identify the types of issues, concerns, and experiences writers write about.

more likely to emphasize a discovery of relationships, associations, and ideas across various aspects of knowledge and information. These relationships enlarge one's perspective, cognition, and awareness of interdisciplinary and intradisciplinary understandings. It is often at this level that connections are discovered by having students examine and compare data, facts, and concepts of one topic or discipline with that of another topic or discipline. By asking students to explore these relationships and to identify patterns, a teacher helps to broaden and deepen a student's understanding of and appreciation for the interconnectedness of knowledge.

The Curriculum of Connections extends the focusing questions in the Core Curriculum by asking students to think about, apply, encounter, and interact with the key concepts, principles, and skills in a variety of contexts. To assist students in answering these questions, a teacher must pose several questions: What are the major concepts and principles in the discipline that are related to the topic or unit that is my focal point? What other topics or problems in this discipline or other disciplines address these same concepts and principles? How might I develop a connection between the topic or unit that is my focal point and other topics or problems to encourage a deeper understanding of the concepts and principles that connect them?

Again, paying close attention to the purpose, characteristics, and student questions of the parallel, teachers can begin the process of formulating Curriculum of Connections ideas for their units of study. The purpose, characteristics, and focusing questions of the Curriculum of Connections are listed in Figure 2.3.

Figure 2.4 shows a template that has been used to brainstorm some potential ideas for a Curriculum of Connections lesson or unit using the charts in Figure 2.3. These curricular suggestions help students to deepen their understanding that (1) writers' voices reveal much about their identities; (2) voice reflects culture, personality, time, and opinions of the writer; and (3) voice is both influenced by and an influence on literary form. These suggestions also require students to read and write a variety of poems, apply understandings about voice and identity to elicit a reader response, and compare and contrast varied forms of writing.

By using the purposes, characteristics, and focusing questions of the Curriculum of Connections, a teacher can refine an existing unit or create a new unit of study. What is most important to remember when filling out the template for the Curriculum of Connections is to return to the existing principles, concepts, and skills that were generated for the unit of study. These ideas are continuously explored in greater depth and complexity as a student works within each parallel. In this parallel, students will be required to use what they know about the topic or disciplinary ideas and skills to further explore how these ideas or skills are carried out in other cultures or during different time periods. Or they may be asked to explore how the ideas, events, or themes are influenced by various conditions (e.g., cultural, political, economic, social, etc.) and/or viewed through the eyes of various people who affected the ideas. There are many connections that can be made within a unit of study, but the purpose of the connections that are being forged should be meaningful in illustrating how things relate, why they are related, and the examples and nonexamples of these relationships. A new appreciation for how knowing these

Figure 2.3   The Curriculum of Connections' Purpose, Characteristics, and Focusing Questions

---

Purpose of the Curriculum of Connections

This parallel is designed to help students discover and learn from the interconnectedness of knowledge. It builds directly on and extends the Core Curriculum. It asks students to see how particular concepts, principles, and/or skills are manifested in other facets of a discipline, across disciplines, in other times or time periods, in other places, or in some combination of those possibilities. It may also ask students to look at how the concepts or skills influenced and are influenced by various people, varying perspectives, and/or different conditions (e.g., economic, political, social, or technological circumstances).

Characteristics of the Curriculum of Connections

The Curriculum of Connections helps students to do the following:

- Discover key ideas in multiple contexts and their similarities and differences
- Apply skills in varied contexts, becoming familiar with both implicit and explicit differences in applications that allow the learner to modify his or her approach in productive ways
- Use ideas and information from one context to ask more fruitful questions about other contexts
- Use ideas and information from multiple contexts to generate new hypotheses or theories
- Make analogies or other comparisons between and among contexts to extend understanding
- Develop ways to see unfamiliar things in familiar ways
- Develop an awareness of an appreciation for multiple perspectives on issues and problems
- Understand the role of individuals in the evolution of the disciplines and of the issues embedded in the disciplines
- Evaluate the relative strengths and weaknesses of various approaches to problems and issues taken by various individuals with varying perspectives

Questions That Students Ask in the Curriculum of Connections

In the Curriculum of Connections, students ask the following questions:

- What key concepts and principles have I learned?
- In what other contexts can I use what I have learned?
- How do the ideas and skills I have learned work in other contexts?
- How do I use the ideas and skills to develop insights or solve problems?
- How do different settings cause me to change or reinforce my earlier understandings?
- How do I adjust my way of thinking and working when I encounter new contexts?
- How do I know if my adjustments are effective?
- How does looking at one thing help me to understand another?
- Why do different people have different perspectives on the same issue?
- How are perspectives shaped by time, place, culture, events, and circumstances?
- In what ways is it beneficial for me to examine varied perspectives on a problem or issue?
- How do I assess the relative strengths and weaknesses of differing viewpoints?
- What connections do I see between what I am studying and my own life and times?

---

connections develops more expertise within a discipline or provides a new sense of familiarity of how an idea is played out in another context or discipline.

USING THE CURRICULUM OF PRACTICE'S PURPOSE, CHARACTERISTICS, AND QUESTIONS TO GUIDE CURRICULAR DECISIONS

The Curriculum of Practice is derived from and extends the Core Curriculum. Curricular activities using this parallel ask students to function with increasing skill

Figure 2.4 A Template for Getting Started With the Curriculum of Connections

Pose Focusing Questions

Ask students the following:

- What universal ideas do writers write about?
- In what literary forms are these universal ideas or perspectives revealed?
- How does voice reflect the culture, personality, time, and opinion of the writer?
- How are perspectives shaped by time, place, culture, events, and circumstances?
- What connections do you see between what you are studying and your own life and times?
- How does understanding the time, culture, and political views of a piece help a reader to understand the elements or traits of a writer?

Generate or Add Activities to Current Curriculum

Ask students to do the following:

- Select a topic of interest to you that is universal enough to be generously represented in varied forms of writing (e.g., love, death, prejudice, injustice, joy, discouragement, conflict).
- Find at least two poems and at least three other forms of writing (e.g., new stories, excerpts from plays or movies, short stories, letters, selections from novels) that represent very different time periods, political views, cultures, and/or personal perspectives.
- Next create a profile (using the same grid format that we practiced to organize your thinking) of the people whose work you chose, showing their characteristics or elements, as well as the excerpts on which you base your conclusions.
- Finally, working alone or with a partner, develop a piece of prose with a piece of poetry embedded in it to explore the following statement:

    We write our lives. It is the subject through which we discover the life we live. In writing, we become teachers about our niche in the universe.

Create Interest/Independent Options

Ask students to do the following:

- Research the work of a poet during one of our historical eras (Civil War, the Great Depression, the American Revolutionary War, the Salem Witch Trials, etc.).
- Gather as many reliable primary resources as you can to show how this poet reflected the times, the events, the issues and concerns. Explain the voice he or she expressed during this time period and identify if it ever changed during the course of the event.

Consider Introductory Activities

- Discuss with students the elements and traits of a writer that his or her writing reveals from previous lessons in the Core Curriculum.
- Ask students to select a variety of poems about war from different times, cultures, and political perspectives to "profile" the authors. Have students create data charts to compare and contrast these poems to look for similarities and differences in the authors' identities. Have students gather evidence (text references) and draw conclusions about what these authors' voices reveal to readers about different times, political views, cultural perspectives, and/or personal perspectives.

Develop Journal Prompts

Ask students to do the following:

- Explain how a writer's early life (including family background and experience, culture, economics, geography, and time) influences his or her voice.
- Explain how a writer's voice could help readers to understand a particular time period, its cultural beliefs, the political climate, or the importance of a particular event.
- Consider whether all writers view things in the same ways. Explain and provide examples of why it would be important to hear from a variety of voices that describe a particular event, the cultural and social perspectives of an issue, or the expressions of voices of those who live during periods of political and religious unrest.
- Look through the writings of poets in the folder that I have created for each of you. Identify with one of the writer's voices. Interpret his or her voice and then apply it to your own creation.
- Consider how it is possible that a particular voice or perspective seems to reveal itself across time and across culture. Generate a list of factors or influences that may help us to understand how this is possible.
- Remember that in many activities, you have identified a writer's voice within a particular piece of poetry. In what other disciplines do you think it important to identify a writer's voice?

Try a Different Teaching Strategy

In order for students to examine the interconnectedness of the ideas presented in this unit, there is a need for me to use better Socratic questioning and deductive logic as scaffolds to help them make connections among the factors that influence and/or shape a writer's voice. I will have students gather evidence in the text that they read and assist them in interpreting these passages. These passages may reveal a writer's beliefs and perspectives in light of the time period the writing reflects. It will also be important to assist students in categorizing this evidence to help them understand that

- Show how your poet's perspectives differed from those of others who held different views of events before or after the event.
- In examining the voice behind the poet, try to provide any evidence you can to explain how your poet's voice shaped or was shaped by any of these factors: culture, geography, economics, political forces, and/or religious beliefs.

Upgrade Products/Assessments

Using several of the elements listed under the Characteristics of the Curriculum of Connections, listed in Figure 2.3, I have decided to upgrade my products to be more reflective and responsive to the suggestions. Some examples follow:

- Create graphic displays of the patterns you have identified across topics, events, and people. These displays can be used to determine the level of instruction that is further required for the student to proceed toward expertise.
- Locate the work of some writers whose voices reflect a universal topic or theme. Students will be asked to gather evidence of how these voices reflect the times, culture, and varying perspectives of the author and the characteristics and traits that are used by the writers to express their voice. In some cases, students will need assistance in planning how to accomplish this learning task. This open-ended task should help me to identify which students need a graphic organizer to help accomplish this task and which others can be asked to create some form of organizing chart to share their results.
- How students respond to the quote will illustrate the degree to which transfer of the unit's principles and concepts has occurred. If students struggle with the interpretation, other quotations can be substituted. It is also possible to have some students locate more difficult quotations to accomplish the same task.
- A rubric will guide students' understanding of the criteria used to judge the level of expertise and conceptual application of the unit's key ideas and skills as they write their essays. This rubric will be used to guide students' performances.

the passages might refer to a writer's belief or disbelief, approval or disapproval of a cultural, political, economic, geographical, or social perspective. The following focusing questions of the Curriculum of Connections assist me in using Socratic questioning: What voice does the writer reveal? Is the voice a reflection of the writer's response to any of the following classifications of influences: cultural, political, geographical, economic, social, or religious perspectives?

Evaluate Current Curriculum

When I used the characteristics of the Curriculum of Connections to view the current curriculum I offer students, my existing unit revealed the following:

Students are simply asked to identify a writer's voice and to determine what factors shape or influence these voices.

The objectives require students to identify the theme that the poet's voice addresses and how the voice reflects a perspective, but they do not require students to apply what they have learned about the principles and concepts of voice and identity to what another writer says about the act of writing.

My curricular tasks of the past have not required students to actively search for other writers who represent different times, cultures, and perspectives or asked students to identify the characteristics and elements that were used by these writers to reflect their voice. This new focus will allow me to ask students to apply and transfer these understandings when studying historical perspectives and how the voice of the narrator typically tells the story.

and confidence, as professionals in a discipline would function. This parallel exists for the purpose of promoting expertise as a practitioner and/or scholar of the discipline. Focusing questions in the Curriculum of Practice ask students to engage in the work of professionals and also to examine the habits, affect, and ethics that guide their work.

We have found that teachers who are most comfortable in using this parallel in their curricular planning typically have experience or expertise in a particular discipline. At times, it is difficult for educators to admit that our level of expertise in this area is not as developed as we would like. One way to deal with this struggle is to initiate conversations with practicing professionals to find out the type of work that they do and the skills that they use to guide their daily work. The use of the Internet has facilitated a wealth of references and curricular materials to assist teachers in becoming more accomplished in knowing how various disciplinarians study their fields and what issues or ideas they explore in their work. For example, when planning to assist students in becoming historians, a typical search engine such as Google can instantly locate information for a teacher about the tools or methods that these researchers use. By simply entering into the search box phrases such as "historical research methods," "thinking like a historian," or "how to analyze primary documents," curricular materials surface from the Library of Congress and other historical agencies that have created Web sites specifically designed to assist teachers in learning the historical tools or obtaining lessons that can be easily modified for classroom use.

The Curriculum of Practice recognizes that each discipline has it own way of behaving, acting, and viewing the world. Understanding that each discipline has a set of lenses, methods, and instrumentation to capture data that reflect everyday experiences and phenomena is the key to unlocking the intent behind the Curriculum of Practice. The purpose, characteristics, and student questions of this parallel (see Figure 2.5) reflect this mission. Figure 2.6 illustrates how our exemplar, the poetry unit, has been shaped using some of these suggestions.

When using the purpose, characteristics, and student questions charts to design curriculum, a teacher will note that not all recommendations are addressed within a unit of study. One must select those items that are an appropriate match for the students for whom the unit is designed. The challenge for elementary teachers is to consider how to introduce these skills and concepts to their students at an early age by designing activities that reflect the authentic nature of the discipline. For middle school and high school teachers, the challenge in using this parallel is to find ways within the school schedule to arrange for student learning experiences that combine the content that they teach with the understanding of how a disciplinarian functions in creating this knowledge.

USING THE CURRICULUM OF IDENTITY'S PURPOSE, CHARACTERISTICS, AND QUESTIONS TO GUIDE CURRICULAR DECISIONS

The Curriculum of Identity is designed to help students see themselves in relation to the discipline, both now and with possibilities for the future; understand the discipline more fully by connecting it with their lives and experiences; increase awareness of their preferences, strengths, interests, and need for growth; and think about themselves as stewards of the discipline who may contribute to it or through it, or both. The Curriculum of Identity uses curriculum as a catalyst for self-definition and self-understanding, with the belief that by looking outward to the discipline, students can find a means of looking inward.

Figure 2.5   The Curriculum of Practice's Purpose, Characteristics, and Focusing Questions

---

Purpose of the Curriculum of Practice

This parallel is designed to help students extend their understandings and skills in a discipline through application of those understandings and skills in ways as much as possible like those of a professional in that discipline. Activities and tasks focus on and guide the student in the journey from novice to expert production in a field. In the process, students are asked not only to engage in the work of professionals but also to examine the habits, affect, and ethics that permeate the work.

Characteristics of the Curriculum of Practice

The Curriculum of Practice helps students to do the following:

- Experience learning in context
- Expand their experiences in the field, leading to greater comfort and confidence in, and identification with, the field
- Develop practical clarity about the key concepts and principles of the field
- Develop awareness of and ways of identifying problems in the field
- Organize their understandings in ways useful for accessing information and for thinking about and acting upon tasks, problems, and dilemmas in the field
- Recognize key features of a variety of problems in the field
- Distinguish and develop meaningful patterns of information in the field
- Distinguish between relevant and less critical information for particular tasks in the field
- Develop fruitful strategies for addressing problems in the field
- Monitor their thinking and problem-solving strategies effectively
- Become acquainted with, and ultimately responsible for, the use of resources and methods that professionals in the field use to teach themselves
- Expand their fluency and flexibility as problem solvers in the field
- Establish awareness of indicators of quality in the field, including those that distinguish between competence and expertise or elegance in the field
- Develop and pursue a sense of the possibilities that the field holds for them as individuals
- Develop awareness of where practitioners work and how those settings affect both the nature of the work and the practitioner

Questions That Students Ask in the Curriculum of Practice

In the Curriculum of Practice, students ask the following questions:

- What are the theories that govern the knowledge of the field?
- How do practitioners organize their knowledge and skill in this field?
- How do the concepts and principles that form the framework of the discipline get translated into practice by those in this field?
- What are the features of routine problems in the field?
- How does a practitioner know which skills to use in given circumstances?
- What strategies does a practitioner use to solve nonroutine problems in the discipline?
- What tools does a practitioner use in his or her work?
- How does one gain access to and skill in using those tools?
- How does a practitioner sense if approaches and methods are effective in a given instance?
- What constitutes meaningful evidence versus less significant information in this field or instance in the field?
- On what basis does a practitioner in the field make educated guesses?
- On what basis does a practitioner in the field draw conclusions?
- What are the methods used by practitioners and contributors in the field to generate new questions, to generate new knowledge, and to solve problems?
- What personality traits support productivity in the field?
- What drives the work of practitioners in the field?
- What are the indicators of quality in the field?
- According to what standards does the field measure success?
- What are the ethical issues and standards of the field?

Figure 2.6   A Template for Getting Started With the Curriculum of Practice

Pose Focusing Questions

Ask the students the following questions:

- What literary or poetic devices do writers use to convey their messages?
- What do writers say about how they write and how they feel about their work as writers?
- What processes do writers use to create their work?
- What do writers' voices reveal to us about social issues? How are these messages interpreted? How does the use of literary devices assist readers' response?

Generate or Add Activities to Current Curriculum

Ask students to do the following:

- Select a poet whose work you find interesting and about whose writing processes you can also find information. Profile the author so you are clear on key elements or characteristics of his or her identity. Also, identify literary or poetic devices this writer uses to convey his or her messages.
- Next take this new information and develop a multimedia project (I-Movie) to share the results of your investigation.
- Finally, compare your analysis with that of five other members of your class. Draw some comparative conclusions about your research. Do all writers create in the same manner? Do all writers share the same dispositions and habits?

Create Interest/Group Investigation

Topic: Looking at Modern America Through Poetry

Instruct students in the following way:

You have learned that poets reflect their attitudes and beliefs about certain issues through the common use of literary elements found in their poetry. With better understanding of these elements, a reader learns to appreciate poetry more because he or she can interpret the messages more clearly. You have also discovered that many poets use poetry as a vehicle for social communication as reflected in the poems they write and views on society and culture they express.

1. Your task is to work within a team to investigate how Modern American poets employ the structural elements of poetry to reflect their attitudes toward modern society and culture. Your team will be assigned a Modern American poet (Langston Hughes, Carl Sandburg, Gwendolyn Brooks, T. S. Eliot, or Edna St. Vincent Millay). Your team's task is to reveal any general themes or attitudes emphasized in the poems to gain a clearer realization of the poet's messages to the audience. By analyzing, studying, and interpreting his or her poetry and researching the poet's life and experiences, you can uncover his or her perspective on modern American society.
2. Team presentations will provide an interpretation of this poet's work, sharing two poems by your assigned poet. You are to draw attention to any literary elements that were used in the poetry, share the poet's perspective on society and culture of America, and explain how the poet revealed this perspective.

Consider Introductory Activities

Read aloud the work of several authors who talk about why they write poetry, how they write poetry, and how they feel about their work as writers. Ask students to identity the elements, traits, and habits of these writers.

Develop Journal Prompts

Ask students to do the following:

- Explain how literary devices can assist a reader in interpreting poetic expression. Use one of the selected poems you have read this week to explain your response.
- Compare the writing style and the processes you use with those of the writers you have read about.
- What have you learned about the traits of various writers that appeal to you as a writer? Which traits are you uncomfortable with? Respond to these questions using any of the literary devices that we have explored in this unit.

Try a Different Teaching Strategy

Within this section of the instructional unit, I am going to move forward in having students conduct group research. My students have not had a great deal of experience with this type of research, so I will use research teams to facilitate the process. An outline of the research steps to guide the process will assist the students in managing their time, understanding how to establish group goals, and creating a list of steps to guide their investigations.

To assist the students in locating resources that they can use to locate information, I will use the Filamentality Web site (www.kn.pacbell.com). This site allows me to locate resources that students can use under one Web address. At any point in the research, students can access this site to locate information and poems of the poets that they are investigating.

The librarian has agreed to compile a list of reference materials that the students can use. Resources (print and media) will be placed on a rolling cart in the library for student use.

I have also located Web sites that address literary criticism. I have located these sites for students to use as their expertise grows. I can use some of these sites for those students who are ready for this level of expert work. The skills offered at these Web sites are those typically used by college students in literary criticism courses.

Upgrade Products/Assessments	**Evaluate Current Curriculum**
Using several of the elements listed under the Characteristics of the Curriculum of Practice, listed in Figure 2.5, I have decided to upgrade my products to be more reflective and responsive to the suggestions. Some examples follow:	When I used the characteristics of the Curriculum of Practice to view the current curriculum I offer students, my existing unit revealed the following:
• Group investigations will take place to address the curricular goals. Realizing that this research task is rigorous, I plan to devote considerable in-class time hosting small group seminars to work with the various teams. Research process guides and rubrics will be distributed to facilitate the management of the learning experiences.	My district curriculum includes little about what writers say about their writing. Students have been asked to interpret and identify a writer's perspective, but the district has not suggested that students understand how voices of writers can be studied to reveal perspectives about social issues during specific times. As I look at my history standards, I notice references to skills that I can use to enhance my unit and help students see the connections between literature and history. I also want to visit the history teacher to see if we can make the group investigation a collaborative project for the students to complete.
• Using the research skills of data collection, analysis, text interpretation, literary criticism, and identification of trends and themes within text, students are learning how to apply the skills of the discipline to draw conclusions about the society and culture of America.	
• Students analyze what writers say about the processes they use as they write. In reading these essays, students begin to comprehend the daily lives of workers or professionals in a discipline; the working conditions, habits, thinking and writing processes, and the intellectual and emotional struggles they encounter. Journal entries, the comparative research project, and profiles should reflect these new understandings.	For years, I have collected books and articles that discuss what writers say about their writing. I will photocopy these and place them in folders for student use when they are asked to analyze what writers say about the process of writing. I will also look through other literature textbooks (that are in the storage room) for support materials that address the curricular ideas that I have generated.

The purposes, characteristics, and focusing questions in Figure 2.7 reflect how these goals can be addressed in a curricular unit. Figure 2.8 illustrates how these recommendations can assist educators in planning curricular experiences that ask students to think about themselves as they reflect on disciplinary perspective.

Educators spend their lives planning curriculum and instruction that is relevant to their students' lives, and I have come to the conclusion that we never really "arrive" at the ultimate level of possibilities. We invite teachers to use this curricular strategy as they begin to shape curricula that reflect the varied purposes, characteristics, and student questions in four parallels of the PCM. The goal is to continually refine classroom lessons so that they assist students in deepening and broadening their understanding of important ideas and skills within a discipline. The template suggested is one way to assist you as a curriculum planner. Use the template in the fashion that we have mentioned, or modify the boxes to reflect other curricular decisions that you deem important to your unit of study.

CONCLUSION

At the beginning of this chapter, I described a young man named Sam, who influenced me greatly in my thinking about curriculum. He taught me many things,

Figure 2.7   The Curriculum of Identity's Purpose, Characteristics, and Focusing Questions

---

Purpose of the Curriculum of Identity

This parallel exists to help students think about themselves, their goals, and their opportunities to make a contribution to their world—now and in the future—by examining themselves through the lens of a particular discipline. The curriculum helps integrate cognitive and affective development.

Characteristics of the Curriculum of Identity

The Curriculum of Identity helps students to do the following:

- Sample the discipline in order to understand themselves in relation to it
- Project themselves into the discipline both intellectually and through working like a practitioner
- Develop an appreciation of the potential of one or more disciplines to help people—including themselves—make sense of their work and live more satisfying and productive lives
- Recognize connections between their own cultural heritage and the evolution of the field, past and future, as well as connections between their cultural heritage and their interests in the field
- Reflect on and identify their skills, interests, and talents, as they relate to one or more disciplines
- Understand how they might shape and be shaped by ongoing participation in a discipline
- Develop a clear sense of what types of lives practitioners and contributors to a discipline lead on a day-to-day, as well as a long-term, basis
- Explore the positive and negative impacts of the discipline on lives of people and circumstances in the world
- Examine their own interests, ways of thinking, ways of working, values, ethics, philosophy, norms, and definitions of quality by examining those things as reflected in the discipline
- Understand the excitement people in a discipline have about ideas, issues, problems, and so on, and how those inquiries energize contributors to a discipline
- Understand the role of self-discipline in practitioners and contributors to the discipline and reflect on the evolving self-discipline of the student
- Think about how creativity is manifest within the discipline so that it helps the student understand his or her creativity
- Develop both a sense of pride and a sense of humility related to self and the discipline that relate to accomplishments, both past and future

Questions That Students Ask in the Curriculum of Identity

In the Curriculum of Identity, the students ask the following questions:

- What do practitioners and contributors in this discipline think about?
- To what degree is this familiar, surprising, and/or intriguing to me?
- When I am intrigued by an idea, what do I gain from that, what do I give as a result of that, and what difference does it make?
- How do people in this discipline think and work?
- In what ways do those processes seem familiar, surprising, and/or intriguing to me?
- What are the problems and issues on which practitioners and contributors in this discipline spend their lives?
- To what degree are these problems and issues intriguing to me?
- What is the range of vocational and avocational possibilities in this discipline?
- In which ones can I see myself working?
- What difficulties do practitioners and contributors in this discipline encounter?
- How have they coped with the difficulties?
- How do I think I would cope with them?
- What are the ethical principles at the core of the discipline?
- How are those like and unlike my ethics?
- Who have been the "heroes" of the evolving discipline?
- What are the attributes of the "heroes"?
- What do I learn about myself by studying them?
- Who have been the "villains" of the evolving discipline?
- What are the attributes of the "villains"?
- What do I learn about myself by studying them?
- How do people in this discipline handle ambiguity, uncertainty, persistence, failure, success, collaboration, and compromise?
- How do I handle those things?
- What is the wisdom this discipline has contributed to the world?
- How has that affected me?
- To what degree can I see myself contributing to that wisdom?
- How might I shape the discipline over time?
- How might it shape me?

Figure 2.8   A Template for Getting Started With the Curriculum of Identity

Pose Focusing Questions

Ask students the following:

- What do practitioners and contributors in this discipline think about? To what degree is this familiar, surprising, and/or intriguing to you?
- What traits and habits of writing do you appreciate? Which traits and habits do you dislike? How does this compare to some of the writers you have read about?
- As you have found out, poets, like all writers, convey their perspectives through the voices they use in their writing. What is your writing voice? What issues would you like to address, and/or what issues concern you enough to develop a strong voice?

Generate or Add Activities to Current Curriculum

Instruct students in the following way:

By reading a series of poets, Jack, the character from *Love That Dog,* not only discovered what he dislikes and appreciates in poetry, but also discovered much about his own identity and voice. You can learn more about your own likes and dislikes by doing the following:

1. Find a piece of literature (fiction, poetry, drama, nonfiction) that reflects an idea or opinion that strongly mirrors your own.
2. Recraft the piece in any way necessary to better reflect not only your voice but also your identity—including time, culture, personality, and values.
3. Select a format to specify what you are learning about yourself through writing and about examining the life and work of writers as well as their characteristics. In other words, what are you finding out about yourself by reflecting on what you have learned about these writers?

Create Interest/Independent Options

Ask students to do the following:

Select one writer whom you greatly admire, one who intrigues you or challenges your perspectives. Find biographical references to this writer and learn more about his or her life. Locate evidence that contributes to your understanding of the problems and issues he or she has spent a lifetime working on. Profile this individual by using prose and poetry selections within your writing. Then reflect on what you have learned about yourself by learning more about this person.

Upgrade Products/Assessments

To upgrade my curriculum, I will offer the following opportunities to the students:

- Ask students to create self-reflection essays that compare their interests, preferences, and strengths with those of practitioners of the discipline.
- Ask students to initiate self-designed projects or products that help them communicate their understanding about themselves as writers.
- Ask students to create analysis charts that show reflections of and reactions to the impact of the discipline on the lives of others in the wider world.

Consider Introductory Activities

- Read selected poetry that reflects you (the teacher) as a writer. Students are asked to identity the elements within the selections that provide clues as to why the teacher selected these pieces.
- Next brainstorm with students how poetry can affect its audience. Generate a list of reasons why different people identify with various poets' works.
- Compare these reasons with other literary forms of writing.

Develop Journal Prompts

Ask students to consider the following:

- You have read the voices of many writers during this unit. What have you learned about your own voice by studying the voices of others?
- You have read many literary selections during this unit: What particular pieces "spoke" to you? You can consider how a particular writer changed your perspective, the issues that they raised for you, or the manner to which they solidified some of your thoughts about an idea. Identify the selection and explain how it affected you.
- You have read several selections from writers who have discussed their work. In what ways do these processes seem familiar, surprising, and/or intriguing to you?

Try a Different Teaching Strategy

I will use this parallel in conjunction with the other parallel activities that I have selected. I want to let students also generate some of their own possible projects as a self-reflection as they interact with the discipline. I will select a few of the student questions from Figure 2.7 and use them to help students create their individual projects. If students take interest in this option, they can select some of these questions to address in their project.

Evaluate Current Curriculum

When I used the characteristics of the Curriculum of Identity to view the current curriculum I offer students, my existing unit revealed the following:

The purpose, characteristics, and student questions, I must admit, have been superficially addressed in my district curriculum. The intent behind these guidelines has caused me to think carefully about how I craft my lessons and activities. I have taught many students who see themselves as a reflection of a discipline, but I have not given any thought to how this expertise develops. I now feel that my teaching can be an instrument for helping students to think about themselves and their goals and to provide opportunities for them to make a contribution to their world.

including how disciplines serve as windows to our world, the joyfulness of some of their consistencies and predictabilities, that all disciplines have laws to live by, and that to become more expertlike, one has to be willing to see the connection between disciplines and how these lenses help us explain life, work hard, and never stop questioning. I thank Sam and all the other young scholars in the world for setting me straight.

Using the Four Parallel Curricula as a Comprehensive Curriculum Model

Philosophy and Pragmatism

Sandra N. Kaplan

It has been said that a good philosophical argument should be able to be translated into practice. It has also been said that a good pragmatic argument needs philosophical roots. The rationale for using all four Parallel Curricula to construct a qualitatively differentiated curriculum can be argued from both philosophical and pragmatic perspectives. The focus of this essay, then, is twofold. First, it provides a rationale for using all four parallels to create a differentiated curriculum. Second, it includes suggestions to develop a classroom environment and teaching strategies that reinforce the Parallel Curriculum Model (PCM) as described in *The Parallel Curriculum* (Tomlinson et al., 2002) and to support the goals and purposes of each parallel.

THE PHILOSOPHICAL RATIONALE

Curriculum developers—who are thoughtful, skillful, and artful—practice argumentation with themselves and other curriculum developers and writers. The centerpiece of the argument is the curriculum and reasoned discussion regarding why the curriculum includes or excludes specific elements. The curriculum developer should be able to define the relationship between the curriculum and the students who will be learning from it. The curriculum developer should be able to defend the selection of one model of curriculum over another or the combination of one model with another. The justification for using all four parallel curricula to form a single curriculum design requires that one understand the why of the philosophy and the how of the pragmatism underlying this type of design.

Why should a curriculum developer use all four parallels of the PCM as he or she orchestrates learning opportunities for students K–12 and across the disciplines? To answer this question, it is important to recognize the difference between a model and a set of elements or activities. A model represents a comprehensive outline to meet a curricular intent wherein all the parts function together to form a whole. The use of only a part of the model dissipates the intent of the model and diffuses the model's relationship to its goals. The selection and focus on a single parallel to form a curriculum seems to redefine each of the parallels as an activity or short-term learning experience targeted at achieving a particular objective, whereas the inclusion of all four parallels to form a single comprehensive curriculum provides a collection of learning experiences or multiple options directed toward a set of goals. The appropriate use of all four parallels to form a comprehensive curriculum presents students with multifaceted learning experiences that support comprehensive understanding.

The development of a comprehensive PCM unit of study inclusive of all four parallels requires understanding that each of the four parallels has unique features and individual merit. It is also important to recognize that the strength of each parallel is derived from its relationship to and interaction with the other parallels in the curriculum. The four Parallel Curricula are interdependent, and each contributes challenge and opportunity to the others. Curriculum developers continually make decisions about which parallel necessitates primary focus while the other parallels receive attention at a less significant level. To make these important decisions, curriculum developers must have clear and precise criteria against which they can weigh their options. Criteria for determining the emphasis to be given to any one parallel curriculum should include the following:

- Students' needs, abilities, and interests
- Compatibility between the curriculum and local, state, and/or national curricular expectations
- Context or setting in which the curriculum will be taught
- Time allocated to teaching and learning the curriculum
- Resources available to the teacher and students
- Support from administrators, peers, and community members

The following patterns exemplify the many and varied ways in which the four Parallel Curricula can be arranged to form a comprehensive curricular structure. Each pattern represents a response to two basic curriculum development questions: Which of the four parallels should receive the greatest emphasis within the comprehensive curriculum structure, and what order of presentation would best facilitate the interdependence among the four parallels?

Example 1: Diversity Among Students

In the first classroom, there is a wide range of abilities among the 27 Grade 4 students. Most students are at grade level, while a small group of students is below grade level, and an equal-sized number is above grade level. Those who are above grade level demonstrate a high level of sophistication with regard to the Core Curriculum and need to go beyond the Core. To provide ongoing levels of challenge to this small group of learners, the four parallels were used in the order shown in the following diagram. The same diagram illustrates the degree of emphasis given to each Parallel Curriculum to form this unit of study.

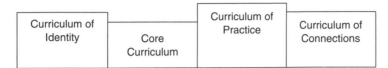

The curriculum developer, in this case the teacher, recognized that understanding of self as a learner could be the motivating factor to engage her above-grade-level students in an area of study previously learned. Therefore, she decided to emphasize the Curriculum of Identity at the outset of these students' experience in the unit. In addition, she decided to emphasize the Curriculum of Practice later in the unit because she felt its focus on the methodology of the field would afford these learners an appropriate level of challenge. In this example, then, the curriculum developer wove together all the parallels in order to meet the unique learning needs of sub-groups of students in the classroom. Her decisions were clearly justified because they were based on an important criterion for determining the appropriate emphasis given to each parallel: an examination of students' needs, interests, and abilities.

Example 2: Connecting Topics of Study

The second example occurs in a middle school context. Eighth-grade students are studying a variety of topics that, at first blush, appear disparate and unconnected: the Industrial Revolution in U.S. history, ecology in biology, and the art of the short story in English, specifically the role of characterization. To unify these seemingly unrelated pieces of the curriculum, the eighth-grade team of teachers decided to emphasize the Curriculum of Connections as a way to "pull together" all three units of study. They selected "change" as a universal concept, and throughout each separate class, they artfully wove into the course of study an examination and discussion of how their topic supported the larger, unifying concept of change: change with respect to American society, change with regard to an ecosystem, and change as it applies to the antagonist of any short story. In essence, these teachers carefully crafted cognitive bridges by emphasizing the goals and purposes of the Curriculum of Connections. The emphasis on this parallel became the catalyst for curriculum investigations for the other three Parallel Curricula. Ongoing assessment revealed that emphasis must be given to the Core Curriculum. Further reflection on the students' interests *and* the goals of the PCM led the teacher to place the Curriculum of Practice and Curriculum of Identity side by side, giving them equal emphasis. This decision was predicated on the fact that these two Parallel Curricula seemed symbiotically related and could reinforce each other, as demonstrated in the following diagram.

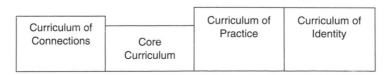

To summarize, the inclusion of the four parallels of the PCM in a single curriculum provides curriculum developers and teachers with a flexible framework to meet both group and individual needs as students progress through their years of schooling. By utilizing all four Parallel Curricula to form a comprehensive curriculum, in either a single classroom or across multiple classrooms, the curriculum developer can respond to the diversity among the individuals or other factors that influence teaching at the classroom level: district standards, time, resources, or administrative support. In addition, this method affords students the opportunity both to sample each parallel curriculum and to engage intensively in a study of one or more of the particular Parallel Curricula.

THE PRAGMATIC RATIONALE

What are some of the practical realities associated with the implementation of PCM? A number of critical decision points exist, and the first has to do with how PCM will be used. Other decision points are related to the classroom environment and the use of aligned pedagogy. Each of these decision points will be discussed in turn.

Add-to, Replace and Integrate, or Extend

Although the PCM can be used as a framework for creating entirely new curricula, it can also be used as a reference to replace or extend components in existing curriculum units. Following are suggestions for possible entry points for using the parallels in combination with existing curricula.

- *Add-to* means that a parallel will become an addendum to some feature of the preexisting lesson.
- *Replace and integrate* means that a parallel becomes a substitute for a feature of the lesson that already has been learned or is not appropriate for learners who may already have mastered portions of the curriculum.
- *Extend* means that a parallel is used to elaborate a feature of the preexisting lesson.

These options are illustrated in Figure 3.1. Remember, the use of any or all of the options is dependent upon the needs, abilities, and interests of students. The Curriculum of Connections may be used, for example, to scaffold an add-to option. The Curriculum of Practice may be used to frame a replacement learning experience for students who have already mastered the Core Curriculum content. Students who are involved with the replacement content focus their work on comparing and contrasting the written work of practitioners in three fields in the social sciences: economics, political science, and sociology. Finally, the Curriculum of Identity may be used to frame an extension for this Core Curriculum writing unit. Students involved in this extension may be those who already demonstrate expertise in writing or appear to have the potential to become a writer.

Building a Classroom Environment

The environment should reflect the curricular and behavioral expectations for the class. Just as advertisements and other artistic renderings direct the attention of the

Figure 3.1 Curricular Application of the Parallel Curriculum

Identifying the Curricular Form	Exploring Options
Standard: Write an essay. **Objective:** Define characteristics of an essay after reading different text materials and then write your own essay. **Materials:** Texts **Motivation:** Discuss difference between *essay* and *story*. **Input:** Define attributes of an essay. **Output:** Write an essay. **Culmination:** Share essays in small groups. **Assessment:** Use rubric.	***Add-to*** **Curriculum of Connections:** Prove with evidence the existence of a relationship between message and media. ***Extend*** **Output:** Write an essay. **Curriculum of Identity:** Define the self as a linguist, essayist, or author. ***Replace and Integrate*** **Output:** Define attributes of an essay. **Curriculum of Practice:** Compare different types and forms of essays related to the disciplines: economics, political science, sociology, etc.

theater patron, the PCM classroom décor should focus the attention of the learner on what is and will be studied. The presence of bulletin boards related to the four Parallel Curricula can set the intellectual stage, so to speak, for what is valued in the classroom. The bulletin boards are reference points for validating what the learner has or will be accomplishing. Figure 3.2 illustrates three examples of bulletin boards that are intended to spark interest in and support the learning of the four Parallel Curricula.

Learning Centers

A learning center is a site within the classroom for students to learn independently or in small groups. The purpose of learning centers is to allow students to develop self-directedness and to acquire the skills of learning-to-learn. Learning centers can be used to introduce new academic content and skills, to reinforce content and skills previously learned in either teacher-directed or student-centered situations, and to extend and enrich content, skill-learning opportunities, or both.

Figure 3.2   Bulletin Boards That Support the Four Parallel Curricula

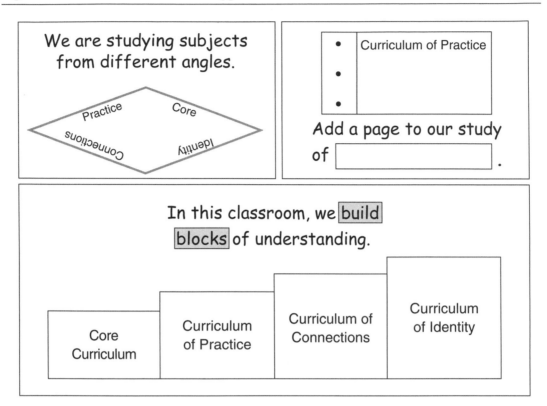

Regardless of the type of learning centers provided to students, it is essential that students understand when and how to use these areas for study. Some educators assign students to a specific time to work at the learning center. Other teachers state that the rotation of groups at the learning center is more equitable, and still other educators feel that free choice is the most beneficial method to engage students in the learning center. Most important to the success of learning centers is the fact that they must be introduced to the students by teachers in a manner that enables learners to thoroughly comprehend the academic, social, and personal responsibilities and expectations related to their use.

A major benefit of using learning centers as a curricular opportunity is that they can provide the reinforcement and extension activities needed to further the understanding of the four Parallel Curricula and how they interact and influence each other. Following is an example of a learning center specifically designed to facilitate the content and skills inherent in the study of the four parallels (see Figure 3.3). The task cards on the completed bulletin board (see Figure 3.4) articulate the activities for students to pursue, and the materials on the table provide the resources needed to complete these activities. The task cards (see Figure 3.5) are open ended and can be applied to any Core Curriculum content illustrated as a border on the bulletin board.

Pedagogy

The existence of various models of teaching for different outcomes has been researched and included in the literature on "best practices." Best practices suggest that student learning is enhanced with the alignment of content and pedagogy.

Figure 3.3   Outline of a Learning Center

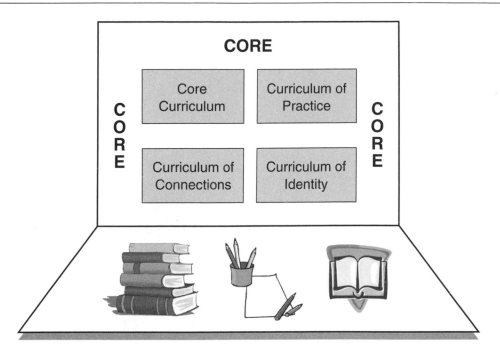

Figure 3.4   Completed Learning Center Highlighting Activities and Resources

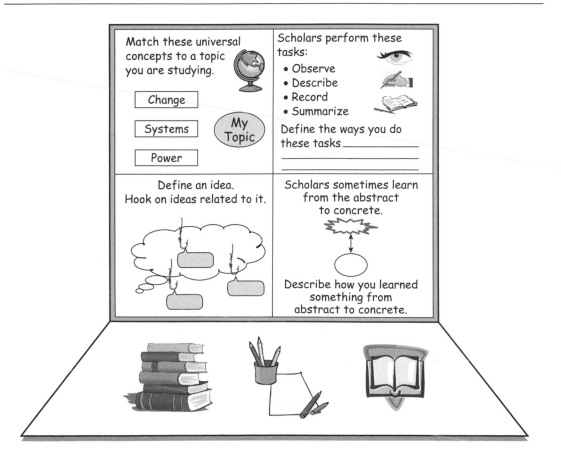

Figure 3.5   Some Additional Task Cards to Use at a PCM Learning Center

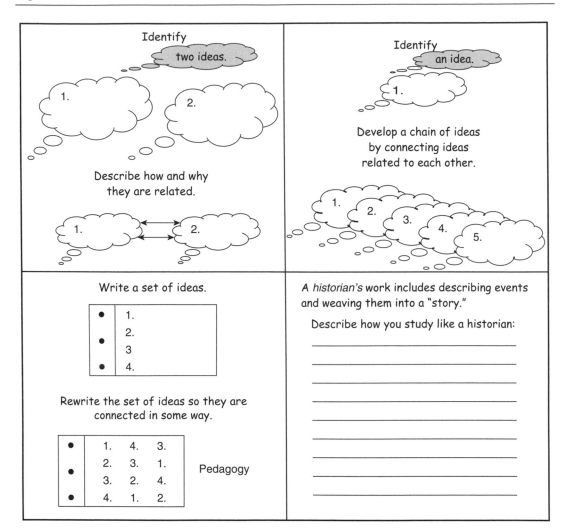

Sometimes a discrepancy exists between what is understood about pedagogy in theory and what is actually practiced in classrooms. Often this is a result of the use of the wrong model of teaching to attain the designated objective. For example, the Six-Step Lesson Plan or Direct Instruction Model (see Joyce & Weil, 1996) has been identified as the model "most used and abused." This model is used to teach students how to accomplish something: how to write an essay, how to compare two areas by assessing likenesses and differences, or how to draw a castle. However, this model is not an appropriate choice of pedagogy to help students understand a principle such as "all change results in positive and negative effects."

Although the Direct Instruction Model is not always the most appropriate model of instruction to use, it is the model most widely used and, in many districts and schools, the only model of teaching that is generally deemed acceptable. Following is an example of how the Direct Instruction Model of teaching may be redesigned to accommodate the inclusion of all four parallels.

The alignment of the four Parallel Curricula to appropriate models of teaching enhances students' abilities to achieve stated outcomes at a level commensurate with the intent of each parallel and their own abilities. Figure 3.6 includes examples of

Figure 3.6   Aligning Content and Pedagogy

	Core Curriculum	*Curriculum of Connections*	*Curriculum of Practice*	*Curriculum of Identity*
Major intent of the parallel	To emphasize the structure of the discipline: its essential concepts, principles, skills, and dispositions	To extend learning using related macroconcepts across settings, times, and circumstances	To promote expertise as a practitioner of the discipline	To help students connect the discipline to self, now and in the future
Aligned pedagogy	• Concept Attainment Model • Inquiry • Simulations • Socratic questioning	• Synectics • Concept Attainment Model	• Strategy-based instruction • Simulation • Inquiry-based instruction • Problem-based learning • Shadowing experiences	• Visualization • Demonstration/ Modeling • Shadowing experiences • Internships • Mentorship
Rationale	Acquisition of concepts and concept categories that are essential to the discipline	Acquisition of concept categories and macroconcepts that support connections between and across disciplines	• Increased ability to solve problems in a field • Increased ability to use the tools and methodology of a discipline	• Increased ability to see oneself as a future participant in a field • Enhanced content area knowledge • Increased understanding of the life of a professional in the field

pedagogical formats that lend themselves to the goals and purposes of each parallel. It is derived from pages 89, 133, 175, and 217 of *The Parallel Curriculum* (Tomlinson et al., 2002).

CONCLUSION

The PCM provides curriculum developers with a flexible framework and four different parallels, which can be used to form a single comprehensive curriculum to provide ongoing and challenging learning experiences for the wide range of learners in today's classrooms. The four parallels can help developers add-to, replace and integrate, and extend curriculum. To decide which parallel(s) to emphasize, when to use them, and with which students, curriculum developers and teachers must consider specific criteria: students' needs, abilities, and interests; local, state, and national curricular expectations; time allocations; resources available; and peer, administrative, and community support.

To maximize the effectiveness of the parallel(s) that will be emphasized, as well as the parallel(s) that will be of less importance in the unit, teachers can build a classroom environment that supports PCM, create learning centers that support all four parallels, and align their teaching strategies with the goals and purposes of the four parallels.

Exploring the Curriculum of Identity

4

Jeanne H. Purcell

Education, in its deepest sense and at whatever age it takes place, concerns the opening of identities—exploring new ways of being that lie beyond our current state. . . . [Education] must strive to open new dimensions for the negotiation of self. It places students on an outbound trajectory toward a broad field of possible identities. Education is not merely formative—it is transformative.

—Wenger, 1998, p. 263

Minnie Johnson's day began at 7:30 A.M. Like every other morning, she had a long list of things to do: check on Miguel, who said he would meet her before class; find a book for the new student; speak to Judy's mother, who is concerned because her daughter failed the last quiz; and talk to the other members of the English department to see how this year's students did on the writing portion of the state assessment. With some of the preparations made for the day, she left the classroom for the main office. The new assistant principle had asked Minnie to help cut the book budget for next year. But today she was distracted by a conversation taking place in the teachers' lounge. It was an animated interchange among her peers about what high school seniors should know and be able to do upon graduation.

A colleague was in the middle of explaining how essential it was that students be prepared to write a coherent essay. "If they can't write, they won't be able to write a report or a letter to an editor."

"I think you are right about that," voiced a new teacher sitting at another table. "In the twenty-first century, students will be living in a vastly more complex world. They will need to be able to read, write, and understand events within the context of the global community. It's most important that today's graduates know the basic skills."

Jake, a veteran colleague, interrupted, "Say what you will. After all is said and done, it just comes down to the fact that we babysit them for a dozen years." The words of her colleagues echoed in Minnie's head. Instinctively she knew that there was something missing in all that she had heard. She began a carefully crafted response.

"It sounds like you have a pretty complete set of goals," she said. "But I think there is one piece missing. You have all talked about the content and skills—writing and computation— but no one has mentioned the students as individuals. I think we want our graduating seniors to have a sense of self: who they have been, who they currently are, and who they are becoming. As much as content knowledge is important, so is each student's emerging identity."

Similar conversations take place (or should take place) in teachers' rooms across the country. In the context of this essay, it serves as a metaphor for the varied perspectives that educators hold about the purposes of education. It suggests that most of our recent attention has been focused on students' acquisition of knowledge and skills. Rarely has mainstream educational reform widened enough to include much emphasis on a student's emerging sense of identity. Without a person like Minnie Johnson to remind us about the affective needs of students, many teachers will unwittingly marginalize students' identities in these complex and demanding times.

This essay is an invitation to teachers to place students' affective needs at the center of their teaching for at least a portion of their time in school. It is also an invitation to broaden our conception of identity development. For much of educational history, identity formation has been equated with career fairs, vocational surveys, take-your-children-to-work days, and the like. The Curriculum of Identity involves much more—the transformation of young people—and invites classroom teachers to become directly involved in the process.

This essay contains two sections. The first section defines the Curriculum of Identity and examines it from three perspectives: (1) as the artful blending of content and affect by the classroom teacher, (2) as a personal storyboard that each student creates across his or her K–12 experience, and (3) as a series of joyful moments that are the cornerstones for each student's personal storyboard. The second section answers the question "What is in it for me?" This question is examined through excerpts from a series of real letters addressed to a teacher from a former student. The letters chronicle the growth of this student from adolescent to adult and father. The recurring themes in the letters—which span more than 20 years—are the young man's deepening sense of self and the impact that the teacher has had on his life. The letters are self-explanatory; they remind us in a compelling way why we all chose teaching as a career and, concurrently, the immeasurable rewards that come to those who attend to students' emerging sense of self.

WHAT IS THE CURRICULUM OF IDENTITY?

The Marriage of Content, Affect, and Intimate Knowledge of the Discipline

As a veteran teacher of English, Minnie has a profound appreciation for literature and for her students. She understands deeply the literary elements at the core of all fiction—characters, plot, theme, setting, mood, foreshadowing—that are used skillfully by writers to craft short stories, novels, and plays. Each year, she carefully selects representative plays, short stories, and novels to illuminate the core knowledge at the heart of literature.

In addition, Minnie has a deep and personal understanding of the role of practitioners in the literary world. As a literature major in undergraduate school, she spent time as an editor in a publishing house. Later in graduate school, she wrote critiques of new fiction books for literary magazines. In her first full-time job, Minnie wrote a weekly news column that featured interviews with local literary figures who wrote short stories, poetry, and historical fiction.

Because of her many experiences, Minnie provides her students with rare glimpses into the lives of practitioners in the discipline. She understands well the issues and problems these professionals face daily. She is well versed about the personal sacrifices—rejection letters, days and weeks of solitude, blank pages, little money, little sleep—that many literary figures endure. She also can relate to her students the tremendous joy and satisfaction that many authors and critics experience when they create a new work that is well received by the public or when they receive acclaim for their craft.

Equally important, Minnie Johnson understands deeply the emotive quality of literature. Young people of all ages love the characters in stories. At the heart of every rich piece of literature are characters whose lives are revealed for readers to admire, scorn, envy, dislike, and even reject. Some of Minnie's most joyful moments occur when she skillfully weds the concepts and principles related to her discipline with the affective needs of her students.

Minnie chooses stories that resonate with adolescents, such as "Stone Boy," by Gina Berriault (2002). In this selection, Arnold, age nine, accidentally shoots and kills his brother, Eugie. Students are always riveted by the horror of the story and the coldness of Arnold's family as they come to terms with Eugie's death. Minnie pauses at teachable moments to ask questions: What is compassion? Understanding? Empathy? How might you have handled Arnold's bid for attention if you had been his mother? His father?

"Thank You, M'am," by Langston Hughes (1991), is another of her favorites. The story provides the perfect context for a discussion about honesty, decision making, and taking responsibility for one's decisions. Poetry provides a distilled and powerful opportunity for students to examine their own lives. Minnie asks students questions such as the following: Why does the narrator pause to reflect in "Stopping by Woods on a Snowy Evening"? What would make you stop to reflect about your own life? Could you devote your life's thinking to metaphors, meter, meaning, and mischief with words?

Minnie's teaching practices are not unique. She has counterparts, across grade levels, who share her sense of responsibility for combining content, affect, and intimate knowledge of the discipline in order to teach about identity formation. In social studies, some teachers emphasize the importance of citizenship, respect for others, conflict resolution, and responsible decision making. Others help students understand the issues and problems faced by those running for public office. In mathematics, there are teachers who emphasize the importance of accuracy and double-checking all answers. Other teachers share with students the nature of some of the unsolved problems that contemporary mathematicians consider. They ask young people to imagine what it might be like to ponder one or two problems for years at a time.

In chemistry, some teachers choose to spend time on a long-term program called "Chemistry on Stage," a nine-week assignment that integrates the historical and scientific components of a scientist's life with an art form—a theatrical performance (Budzinsky, 1995). Students are required to select and portray a prominent figure in the field of chemistry. They conduct research, write a script, and prepare a mini-stage production that includes aspects of the scientist's personal life and professional accomplishments. The performance invites students to reflect on questions such as the following: Do I like the kinds of problems that chemists try to solve? Do I have the commitment and persistence to undertake the problems that chemists solve? How do people in this discipline think and work? Am I willing to make the enormous sacrifices that are required in order to contribute in a substantial way to a field? How might I handle the uncertainty, failures, and successes that chemists experience in their field? What current issues in the field intrigue me? To what degree can I see myself contributing to the knowledge in the field?

Minnie and other teachers in similar situations unite their content, intimate knowledge of the discipline, and the affective needs of their students in a purposeful way. On one level, they teach the essential concepts and principles of their respective disciplines. At the same time, they use their content as a mirror in which students can see themselves, now and in the future. (See Figure 4.1 for a list of focusing questions for the Curriculum of Identity.) In many ways, teachers who employ the Curriculum of Identity accumulate "double mileage" because they focus not only on a content area but also on the identity of their students.

Personal Storyboarding

What is the combined effect of teachers who make students the focus for at least some portion of their teaching? They support the personal story building that is at the heart of the Curriculum of Identity. Taken as a whole, they each contribute to helping a student answer the questions "Who am I?" and "Who might I like to become?"

As early as kindergarten, young children begin to create stories about themselves. Their information is gathered from those closest to them—their parents, other family members, relatives, and teachers. For many very young children, the point of departure for identity formation is awareness of simple physical attributes, such as height, ethnicity, and resemblance to other family members. Parents and teachers can help each young child see how he or she is similar to others and, at the same time, point out and encourage their emerging strengths and interests.

By ten years of age, many upper elementary children are able to move beyond their physical attributes to process more abstract traits, such as interests and goals. Teachers play an important role in advancing children's personal storyboards as they enter this stage of abstract thought. At any time in the course of a curriculum unit, intermediate and middle school teachers can pose questions such as the following to help students reflect on their emerging sense of self: "What disciplines

Figure 4.1   Focusing Questions for the Curriculum of Identity

1. What do practitioners and contributors in this discipline think about?

2. To what degree is this familiar, surprising, and/or intriguing to me?

3. When I am intrigued by an idea, what do I gain from that, what do I give as a result of that, and what difference does it make?

4. How do people in this discipline think or work?

5. In what ways do these processes seem familiar, surprising, and/or intriguing to me?

6. What are the problems and issues on which practitioners and contributors in this discipline spend their lives?

7. To what degree are those intriguing to me?

8. What is the range of vocational and avocational possibilities in this discipline?

9. In which ones can I see myself working?

10. What difficulties do practitioners and contributors in this discipline encounter?

11. How have they coped with the difficulties?

12. How do I think I would cope with them?

13. What are the ethical principles at the core of the discipline?

14. How are those like and unlike my ethics?

15. Who have been the "heroes" of the evolving discipline?

16. What are the attributes of the "heroes"?

17. What do I learn about myself by studying them?

18. Who have been the "villains" of the evolving discipline?

19. What are the attributes of the "villains"?

20. What do I learn about myself by studying them?

21. How do people in this discipline handle ambiguity, uncertainty, persistence, failure, success, collaboration, and compromise?

22. How do I handle those things?

23. What is the wisdom this discipline has contributed to the world?

24. How has that affected me?

25. To what degree can I see myself contributing to that wisdom?

26. How might I shape the discipline over time?

27. How might it shape me?

are represented by this material? Who are some of the 'heroes' in this discipline? What can I learn about myself from studying them? Who are some of the villains? What can I learn about myself from studying them?" When teachers combine content with affect in this way, they provide students with opportunities to refine their emerging identity. The guiding questions for the Identity Parallel (see Figure 4.1), in concert with the content, act as a "springboard" for students to reflect on their own interests, goals, and dreams.

Obvious student strengths, such as a student's love of science or a budding interest in the visual arts, are easy to spot and promote through grade-level curricula. Students are quick to recognize their passionate liking for an area. Evan Feinberg, the National Association for Gifted Children Nicholas Green award winner[1] in 2001, from North Stratfield School in Fairfield, Connecticut, is a case in point. In his essay for this award, this fourth grader wrote clearly about his passions and goals:

> My deep thirst for knowledge has led me to pursue my research in astronomy and even create my own books to share with my family and classmates: *The Eight Books of Space-Time* and *Space Bends While Time Warps: Play With Einstein's Gravity.* . . . My study and research triggered new life goals for me such as being a physicist or a cosmologist, proposing new theories, and aspiring to be like my role models, Stephen Hawking and Albert Einstein. My dream is someday to unlock the ultimate theory of the universe.

Some upper elementary students want to be many things. Areta, a fifth-grade student, said,

> In fifteen years I will be twenty-five and living in Pennsylvania. Fresh out of Princeton, I will be working with my law partner in our small law firm. I will also be working in an acting theater close to home. I will split my time between the firm and the theater where I will teach some classes as well as act in some performances. I will live in an apartment with Casey. Our apartment will be right next door to Dunkin' Donuts.

Geraldo, another fifth-grade student, described the following "future self":

> My dream is to graduate from college and become an MLB catcher for the New York Yankees!! If I don't do that, then I plan on being a scientist like my great uncle. What I never want to do is work at a fast food restaurant or be a teacher (no offense to Ms. Wilken), but I could be a waiter, bartender, or maybe even a chef.

Areta's and Geraldo's teachers have dual challenges when young people see so many possibilities. Not only must they share with Areta and Geraldo the range of vocational possibilities within each discipline mentioned, but they must also show the range of avocational possibilities within the respective disciplines. With this information in hand, students will be able to see many ways of pursuing all their current interests and dreams.

For other upper elementary and middle school students, however, the strengths may not be as obvious. Teachers who make students the focus of their work use their curriculum—in conjunction with their powers of observation—to help students realize their latent abilities and potential areas of strength. Endia, for example, is a quiet but serious fifth grader. Her academic records reveal that she encountered difficulties in second grade when she was retained as a result of a serious illness that kept her out of school. She will shyly reveal—if prodded—that she wants to write a book called "History in the Past and in the Making," which will describe African Americans who have made the world a better place. "My book," she said, "will ask and answer the kinds of questions that aren't included in textbooks." Her teacher does all that she can to support Endia's love for history and writing by helping her understand the concepts and principles that are at the heart of history. This teacher provides Endia with opportunities to write her own histories so that she can experience, firsthand, the way historians think and work.

Equally important, these same teachers realize how vital it is to help the most noninvolved students develop at least a curiosity for a topic or discipline, perhaps even an appreciation over time. Connor is a case in point. Although Connor was a good reader, he disliked anything that required reading. In addition to knowing about his dislike for reading, his teacher knew that he loved sports. To encourage his involvement with reading, she made a point to offer him frequent opportunities to read about sports and sports-related events. Her hope was that she could move him up "one notch" on the engagement continuum (see Figure 4.2). Those who are serious about helping young people create their own storyboard make a concerted effort to learn deeply about each learner in the classroom and provide multiple opportunities—through the curriculum—to encourage nonexistent and emerging strengths and to advance latent strengths.

By middle to late adolescence, many students become capable of a far more differentiated view of self. Each student's personal story becomes complex and multidimensional because the learner sees himself or herself with a variety of traits, abilities, values, goals, dreams, and interests. Although students at this stage may oscillate among competing identities, the range of traits that they exhibit begins to coalesce to reflect a certain kind of person. Teachers attuned to the Curriculum of Identity support students as they "try on" different dreams, interests, professional roles, and life philosophies; reflect upon the "fit"; and make decisions about which

Figure 4.2   Engagement Continuum

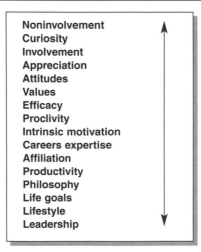

Noninvolvement
Curiosity
Involvement
Appreciation
Attitudes
Values
Efficacy
Proclivity
Intrinsic motivation
Careers expertise
Affiliation
Productivity
Philosophy
Life goals
Lifestyle
Leadership

Figure 4.3   "On the Banks of the Amazon": An Essay by Caitlin Burns

---

I lay sprawled, limbs akimbo, on coarse, cotton sheets. The air hung heavy, seeping through the mosquito netting to kiss my skin, to saturate it with moisture. Above my head, the gauzy canopy glowed in the moonlight dancing off the river, dancing to the symphony of jungle sounds. The shrieks and cries emanating from the brush accompanied a lazy breeze strumming the lianas in the trees. Fighting sleep, I strained to keep my eyes open. To sleep would be to stop hearing the gorgeous music, stop feeling the night air, and stop knowing that I am the luckiest girl in the world. How many thirteen-year-olds have lifelong dreams fulfilled at such a young age? That night I fell asleep on the bank of the Amazon.

Three weeks before I entered high school I had sat on the riverbank watching the stars rise above the water and listening to fishermen play their flutes, notes cast out into the murky deep of the jungle. I saw such beauty in the Amazon, but I saw great sorrow as well. I saw the blood and sweat of Peruvians as they chopped down trees to shelter their families, and the denuded landscape they left behind. I cried as I watched men, struggling to feed their families, cast out round nets again and again, raping the riverbed of all life.

Lying in the Amazon night, I heard strains of music resonating from the docks by the river. I listened sleepily until I became aware of a very different song coming from the opposite direction, coming from the dark recesses of the forest. The cry of the parrot settling down to sleep, the snuffling grunts of a capybara foraging for food, the screech of an agouti being pursued by a predator all intertwined with the fisherman's flute. Listening to the symphony being played simultaneously by human and nature, I wondered: If two such disparate musicians can play so beautifully together in the dark of night, why can they not do the same in the day, when the children must be fed and the huts re-thatched.

I have spent three years pondering the answer. I left the jungle an indignant girl three years ago, determined to save the rainforest. So I took anthropology courses and AP biology; I read books, and I talked to adults in the field of big ideas. I learned about conservation techniques like crop rotation and fish farming. I discovered that there was a field precisely tailored to saving the world. I can go to a reputable university, major in biology and anthropology and with a little luck and hard work, find myself back in the rainforest. There I will be the conductor of the song I heard that night, uniting people and nature in a gorgeous melody that will play on long after I am gone, dawn to dusk on the banks of the Amazon.

---

values, goals, and dreams are "just the right size." Some focusing questions that could be used at this stage of adolescent development include the following: What are the ethical principles at the core of this evolving discipline? How are they like or unlike my ethics? What is the "wisdom" that this discipline has contributed to the world? To what degree can I see myself contributing to that wisdom?

Throughout their adolescence, students make incremental progress toward a true sense of their "future self." Figure 4.3 contains one senior's essay for college and represents the degree of self-knowledge that we would like all twelfth-grade students to possess at the end of their public school experience. "On the Banks of the Amazon," by Caitlin Burns, captures many aspects of this student's personal storyboard: her values and beliefs, as well as her personal vision for whom she will become.

Long-Lasting Joy

What is the driving force behind the personal storyboard? Quite simply, it is joy—long-lasting joy—that students experience when they find a bit of themselves through the curriculum. Sometimes it is joy with a capital *J*, as in the case of students who win the Intel Science Talent Search,[2] for example, or the Nicholas Green Award. For the vast majority of students, however, the joy they find is equally powerful, although on a smaller scale, such as when Caitlin discovered that she wanted to save the rainforests that flank the Amazon River or when a young student discovers that he likes consensus building or problem solving. Some would suggest that these experiences are junior-sized versions of the "flow experience" described by Csikszentmihalyi (1990): "Every flow activity . . . had this in common: a creative feeling of transporting the person into a new reality. It provided a sense of discovery. . . . It transformed the self by making it more complex" (p. 74).

Long-lasting joy galvanizes young people with an activity, a topic, or a field of study and challenges them to their fullest capacity. Because the student feels joy about his or her work, the task or activity becomes intrinsically rewarding. The positive feelings and feedback spur further engagement and higher levels of attainment. Quite simply, long-lasting joy leads to intrinsic motivation and shapes—in a significant way—the student's emerging sense of self (Bandura, 1993; Csikszentmihalyi, 1990; Deci & Ryan, 1985; Goleman, 1995). As long as the emerging sense of identity continues to be perceived as meaningful by the young person, it will continue to be a central shaping force in his or her life (Zuo & Cramond, 2001).

What, then, is the Curriculum of Identity? With respect to the school environment, it is a clear and simple set of interactions. It begins with purposeful actions by practitioners who blend skillfully their content, the affective needs of their students, and their knowledge of practitioners within a discipline. Students respond to these teachers' finely crafted lessons. As they respond to these lessons and are provided with opportunities for reflection about themselves across their school years, they experience joyous moments of self-discovery that help them clarify, with incremental levels of accuracy, their own personal story: who they are and who they might become. The Curriculum of Identity moves us beyond the guidance office door and Career Days. Identity formation, as discussed here, holds tremendous power—life-changing power—that serves to unite teachers in one of the schools' most critical missions.

WHAT'S IN IT FOR ME?

Obvious reasons exist for incorporating the Curriculum of Identity into curriculum units. Systematic use of the Curriculum of Identity can increase student engagement or motivation to learn, increase the likelihood of self-actualization and lifetime productivity, and illuminate powerful differences among students.

Yet what personal benefits accrue to the teacher who elects to incorporate this curriculum parallel into his or her teaching? Quite simply, it makes teaching more enjoyable and satisfying. Teachers report professional satisfaction when they know they have been able to "plant a seed" in the mind of a young child. More tangible evidence comes when teachers receive visits from former students who return to share their accomplishments or receive letters about the difference they have made in students' lives. Following are excerpts from letters from one such student. The excerpts span more than 20 years and serve to remind us about the transformational power—held within this curriculum parallel—that is ours to impart, should we choose the honorable role of steward for other people's children.

April 1980

Dear Mrs. Wilson,

. . . [I]n all, since graduation, 1978, life has been good to me. Most important, my writing has progressed well. I have finally accepted it as my strongest ability and intended fate. With the generous guidance of my new mentor, I've managed to vastly improve my prose. Much remains to be done, and I have given up expecting immediate public gratification. . . . In short, I've been given a talent and a destiny; I intend to fully realize both.

Love and thoughts, Jeff

June 11, 1980

My Dear Mrs. Wilson,

. . . Spring semester at school [Duke University] was hectic and my short vacation has renewed me. I find a new sense of calm, and I am able to spend a couple hours each day writing, then many hours reading: Frost, Tolstoy, O'Connor, McCullen, Eliot, Tyler, Pope, Keats, Wordsworth. . . . I manage to earn enough money to get by.

Love, Jeff

July 5, 1980

Dear Mrs. Wilson,

"Sweetwater," my most recent short story, has been accepted for publication in a fine annual anthology entitled Writers' Forum, a western publication. The publisher has given me high-praise, "You make the West dance, finding, as few others are doing, where the pulse is." Not too bad for a Yale drop out, easterner, huh? The acceptance and praise are very meaningful. Am working on another short story.

Love and thoughts, Jeff

August 30, 1980

My Dearest Mrs. Wilson,

It occurred to me recently that perhaps I have been less than explicit about my debt to you regarding my writing. I've long acknowledged your steady encouragement and understanding, but I'd like to go one step further in recognizing just how important your support of my work has been. Quite simply, you are the oldest and most important direct influence on the development of my writing abilities. You recognized and encouraged my talent long before I knew I had a talent or dreamed of using it. Through my high school years and Yale and Boston, you were the only consistent light in an often dark landscape. I honestly don't know where I would have ended had that light been denied. I can hear your response already. . . . "Jeff, you were destined to write, would have without me." I agree with the first clause of that statement and believe very strongly in my destiny. But destiny can only be achieved through human hands; and in my writing fate, yours have been the most important for the longest period. Verbal thanks for all that seems wholly insufficient, but I offer it anyway and hope you'll let me repay the big debt in other ways on into the future. . . . Have you read my latest short story, "In the Wilderness," yet? Any thoughts?

Love, Jeff

———————————❖———————————

October 1981

Dear Mrs. Wilson,

Enclosed is a copy of the news magazine containing my first publication, duly signed and dated by yours truly. The piece I sent you last, "Four Dreams, Four Wakings," has been accepted for publication in *The Archive*, the college magazine. I am still circulating other short stories. All these pursuits are in keeping with the goal I set for myself. . . .

Love, Jeff

———————————❖———————————

July 1983

Dearest Mrs. Wilson,

And somewhere in all the events of the past, I am engaged! I send my love to you and your new baby. . . .

I'm yours, Jeff

———————————❖———————————

January 1985

I'm still building houses, am now a junior partner in our small company. My "for money" job necessarily impinges on my writing. I've never given up on writing. In fact, it is perpetually alive in me, struggling for expression. The physical demands of carpentry leave too little energy to be both husband and artist. I don't know what all this means. I do think that I will keep on writing, one way or another.

Love, Jeff

———————————❖———————————

April 15, 1987

Dearest Mrs. Wilson,

Income tax day! I wanted to send along these pictures of your brand-new god-daughter. It may seem odd to some that her godparents are neither blood-relatives [n]or live nearby. But those seem superfluous matters to us. . . . While we gave this matter much serious thought, you were our choice from the start.

Love to all, Jeff

————————————❖————————————

December 30, 2002

My Dearest Mrs. Wilson,

I'm writing this from our Virginia cabin along the Blue Ridge. We've had this summer home for a little over a year now and are enjoying its peacefulness and unadulterated natural beauty. It has become my retreat from the frenetic pace of life. I spend more time up here than anyone—sometimes driving up alone from Durham—for a day or two to tend the yard or mow the lawn. It's nice to rediscover solitude and places my mind hasn't wandered for years. Deep within my mind's wanderings, I have discovered a profound need to return to my writing. Life has provided me with so many extraordinary experiences to distill. Destiny is close upon me. . . . Until my next letter from the Blue Ridge. . . .

With love and warmest thoughts, Jeff

CONCLUSION

The Curriculum of Identity is a unique parallel. It is a finely crafted and thoughtful tool that teachers can use to encourage joyful awakenings from students about their emerging sense of identity. In the right hands—hands that are willing to share and to help shape the lives of children—the Curriculum of Identity is the most profound gift a teacher can give a child. Teachers who use this tool will find satisfaction from knowing that they have deeply touched the lives of young people. Hopefully, these teachers will be lucky enough to have at least one "Jeff" in their lives, who—like Minnie—reminds us just why we teach.

NOTES

1.   The NAGC Nicholas Green Distinguished Student Awards are presented annually to one student in grades three to six in each state for excellence in academics, the arts, or leadership. A national award winner is then selected by the Nicholas Green Scholarship Fund from among the state winners. Information about the award is available at www.nagc.org.

2.   The Science Talent Search (STS) is America's oldest precollege science competition. For more than 60 years, this competition—often referred to as the "junior Nobel Prize"—has provided an incentive and an arena for U.S. high school seniors to complete an original research project and have it recognized by a national jury of highly regarded professional scientists. For more information, see www.intel.com/education/sts/

Ascending Intellectual Demand Within and Beyond the Parallel Curriculum Model

Carol Ann Tomlinson,
Sandra N. Kaplan, and Kelly Hedrick

When we do our best thinking as educators, we ask ourselves not only how we can pack more information into learners but how we can ensure that they grow as responsible thinkers, wise consumers of ideas, and innovative contributors to improved conditions for those who share the journey through life. We ask ourselves not just how we can raise test scores but also how we can play a vital role in ensuring that each student becomes all he or she can become.

Such development has to do with knowing, understanding, doing, connecting, contributing, and self-reflection. Those elements are exercised by virtually all human beings at all stages of development, but it should be the case that high school students, for example, are far more sophisticated in understanding how the concept of "scarcity" works in history than would be first graders who encounter the concept of "scarcity" in their early study of economics. It should be the case that middle school learners are more adept at determining which type of thinking to use in a given context than are third graders—but less so, for example, than graduate students.

Such statements are general, of course. No doubt there are third graders with understandings about the solar system that are greater than those of many high school students. There may be adolescents who are far more self-reflective than the adults who work with them.

Both those general statements and the exceptions to them point us toward three important truths. First, as educators, we should proactively attend to the intellectual, affective, and moral development of the young people we teach. Second, those young people will develop at different rates and along different paths intellectually, affectively, and morally. Third, it then becomes our responsibility as educators to meet each learner at his or her current point of development and ensure his or her continual development.

That means we would need to have plans not only for covering the curriculum but also for consistently probing its meaning and implications for young people who are ready to know, understand, do, connect, contribute, and reflect at differing levels of sophistication. It means we would envision each learner on an "escalator of development" and envision ourselves as seeing to it that each escalator moves steadily upward in all those areas required for persistent intellectual, affective, and moral growth in *all* students—and in *each* student.

In the Parallel Curriculum Model (PCM), the concept of Ascending Intellectual Demand (AID) offers a way of thinking about such development. It provides a way of consistently and purposefully refining the match between learner development and curriculum and instruction.

WHAT IS ASCENDING INTELLECTUAL DEMAND?

The PCM takes a firm position that virtually all students should consistently interact with a rich, high-quality curriculum—that is, a curriculum that reflects the nature of the disciplines, is well organized to reveal meaning, engages students, is satisfying, seems purposeful to students, deals with profound ideas, and so on (Tomlinson et al., 2002). Further, the model advocates that this kind of curriculum and instruction should occur in classrooms that feel safe, affirming, and validating for each learner and those that build a sense of the value of each learner, both individually and as members of the group. Teachers in such classrooms consistently reflect on the needs of each student as well as the class as a whole, teach responsively to student need and development, and honor both student differences and commonalities. Among the goals of such classrooms are building student awareness of and respect for their own needs, strengths, ideas, and contributions as well as those of all others in the community of learners and increasing reflection on connections among what students learn, who they are, what they can do, and how they can be contributors to the larger world (Mahoney, 1998; Tomlinson et al., 2002).

Classrooms, curricula, and instruction that support development of these attributes would provide consistent challenge for most learners. A key role of the teacher would be supporting the success of far more learners than is typically the case at this substantial level of expectation. Over time, all learners should move along a continuum toward expertise.

There will also always be students who know more, learn more rapidly, think more deeply, and/or are more innovative in particular domains of study than many of their peers. To maintain escalators of development for these students, teachers need guidelines for extending curriculum in ways that extend the growth of these learners. The concept of AID provides such guidance for teachers, even as it charts a course for all learners in a journey toward ever-increasing proficiency.

One way of envisioning the concept of AID is represented in Figure 5.1. It suggests that, using this concept, teachers would first seek experiences beyond the text

Figure 5.1   Ascending Intellectual Demand: An Overview

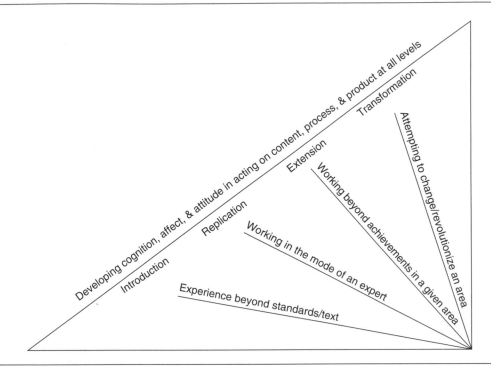

for learners to extend their development. As students are ready, the teacher would increasingly ask them to work in expertlike ways. At some point, certain students will be ready to challenge ideas and achievements in a given area, others to change or even revolutionize an area. At the stage when a teacher introduces AID, as well as at the Replication, Extension, and Transformation stages, the teacher's goal is assisting students in developing their cognition, affect, and attitude by acting on the content of the topic, processes of thought and work, and products students produce to demonstrate and extend their knowledge, understanding, and skill.

HOW DOES ASCENDING INTELLECTUAL DEMAND RELATE TO OTHER GUIDES FOR CHALLENGE?

The need to challenge advanced learners is central to the literature of gifted education and ought to be a part of instructional planning in all classrooms. There are many leaders in the area of curriculum for gifted learners who have provided educators with important ways of thinking about what it means to challenge students whose capacities outstrip general expectations for learners of their age or grade. A few examples of those leaders and some of their ideas regarding challenge for gifted learners follow.

For example, Virgil Ward (1980) suggested that instruction challenging for gifted learners would do the following: emphasize intellectual activity; be flexible; proceed at a pace and level of complexity suited to advanced capacities; be rooted in the theories and concepts of the disciplines; center on acquisition of meaning; be designed to promote inquiry, creativity, and use of scientific methods; draw upon advanced materials; promote personal, social, and civic adequacy; be designed to generate further ideas and development; and assess achievement according to advanced objectives.

George Betts (1985) advocated challenge through facilitating self-esteem and social skills; stressing student interests and open-endedness; helping students grow as independent learners; providing cross-disciplinary learning; stressing a wide array of basic skills as well as higher-level skills; providing broad-based topics with emphasis on major themes, problems, issues, and ideas; providing in-depth learning; developing new products; and participating in cultural activities.

Sandra Kaplan (1994) proposed challenge through development of depth (language of the disciplines, details, patterns, trends, unanswered questions, rules, ethics, and big ideas) and complexity (points of view and interdisciplinary relationships) in various combinations and contexts.

June Maker and Aleene Nielson (1996) suggested challenge through content that is abstract, complex, varied, and economically organized and that studies people and methods key to the disciplines; through process that is high level, is open ended, emphasizes discovery, calls upon students to provide evidence of reasoning, is appropriately paced, and is varied; and products that center on real problems and audiences, call for transformation, are varied, stress self-selection, and are evaluated appropriately.

Carol Tomlinson (1996) proposed "The Equalizer" to depict challenge at increasing levels of transformation, abstractness, complexity, multifacetedness, mental leap, openness, ambiguity, independence, and speed of learning.

Joe Renzulli and Sally Reis (1997) supported challenge through applying student interests, knowledge, creativity, and task commitment to self-selected areas of study; developing advanced-level knowledge of content and methods important to various disciplines and areas of study; developing authentic products for specific audiences; developing skills of self-directed learning; and developing task commitment, self-confidence, and the ability to interact with others.

Joe Renzulli, Jann Leppien, and T. Hays (2000) advocated challenge through applying methodologies of the various disciplines; stressing the key concepts and principles of the disciplines; and applying research methodologies of experts in the disciplines. These approaches lead to emphasis on enduring knowledge, concentration on representative topics, and development of process skills with broad transfer potential.

Joyce VanTassel-Baska and Catherine Little (2003) advised challenge via intradisciplinary and interdisciplinary connections; metacognition; cultivation of habits of mind representative of professionals in a discipline; inquiry and problem solving; new technologies as tools for learning; outcomes of significance; authentic assessment; multicultural and global concerns; concepts; multiple resources that allow flexible, varied, and sophisticated delivery; and substantive content. In addition, there is a long history of literature demonstrating benefits of accelerating the academic progress of advanced learners (e.g., Southern & Jones, 1991).

Each of these approaches to modifying curriculum and instruction in ways that ensure persistent and positive challenge for advanced learners is valuable and can be employed in conjunction with the PCM as well as with other approaches to curriculum design and development. The concept of AID does not supplant other worthwhile approaches to envisioning challenge for advanced learners. Rather, it offers yet another lens for looking at this essential role of teachers who seek to ensure that the capacity of each learner—including those with prodigious abilities—is extended in their classrooms.

HOW IS ASCENDING INTELLECTUAL DEMAND DIFFERENT FROM OTHER APPROACHES TO CHALLENGE?

While the concept of AID is compatible with other approaches to understanding and designing growth-producing challenge for advancing and advanced learners, it differs from other approaches in at least two key ways. Understanding these differences is important to practitioners who want to use AID as a consistent part of instructional planning for advanced learners.

First, AID emphasizes progression toward expertise in one or more disciplinary areas. The PCM itself was developed with intent to guide learners progressively toward expertlike functioning in the disciplines. Each of the model's four parallels provides a different vantage point for learning. To that end, the PCM assists students in developing a conceptual framework of the topics and subjects they study that approximate the conceptual frameworks of experts in those disciplines. The parallels of Connections, Practice, and Identity build upon and extend the conceptual framework of the Core parallel in unique ways—but always with an eye to developing the knowledge, traits, attitudes, and skills of experts. In short, to apply the PCM is to establish for teacher and students expertlike conceptual understandings of areas of study, and then to extend that conceptual foundation. AID likewise exists in large measure to help teachers design curricula that establish and extend expert-focused understandings as particular learners demonstrate readiness for continuing movement toward expertise.

For virtually all learners, curriculum leading toward expertise

- is built on the key concepts, principles, skills, and information of the discipline;
- ensures understanding of the discipline rather than rote memory of information;
- helps students understand problems rather than searching for canned or recipe-like solutions;
- emphasizes depth of knowledge rather than breadth of knowledge;
- helps students seek relevant information from large bodies of information;
- ensures that students know where, when, and why to use knowledge rather than simply repeating it;
- helps students learn to teach themselves;
- encourages students to monitor their approach to problem solving; and
- helps students step back from problems to examine whether the knowledge and processes they are using are appropriate, relevant, and effective (National Research Council, 1999).

To apply AID is to guide all young learners to walk increasingly in the paths of experts. A discussion of what this means when translated into classroom practice follows later in this chapter.

Second, AID differs from previous conceptions of evoking challenge in that it directly addresses the purposes of the four parallels in the model. That is, the Core parallel exists to help learners understand what information means, why it matters, how it is organized, how it makes sense, what it is for, and how the students themselves can use the ideas and skills experts use in a discipline. AID that is focused on the Core parallel should help students answer those questions in greater depth; with more advanced materials; at a brisker pace; at greater levels of depth, abstractness, complexity, or breadth; with more expertlike criteria for quality; with more expertlike patterns of thought and reflection; and so on (Tomlinson et al., 2002).

The Curriculum of Connections is derived from and extends the Core Curriculum, helping learners apply key concepts, principles, and skills across instances in a discipline, across disciplines, across time and time periods, across times and cultures, through varied perspectives, and so on. AID that is applied to the Curriculum of Connections focuses learners on making connections that are markedly unfamiliar to them, establishing defensible criteria for weighing the value of connections, developing solutions that bridge differences in perspectives and still attend meaningfully to problems, searching for connections among apparently disparate areas, looking at interactions among connections, and so on (Tomlinson et al., 2002).

The Curriculum of Practice is also derived from and extends the Core Curriculum. It guides learners in understanding theories that govern the knowledge of experts; translating key concepts, principles, and skills into practice; understanding the routine features of problems with which practitioners in the discipline typically work; determining how practitioners know which knowledge and skill to use in varied contexts; functioning as producers or scholars in the discipline; and so on. AID that is applied to the Curriculum of Practice calls on students to move from expertlike work to expert-level work. In doing so, it guides students in moving beyond addressing routine problems in a discipline to examining and grappling with nonroutine problems, testing their own frameworks of knowledge and skill through repeated field-based tasks, assessing their best work against exemplars of best quality from experts in the discipline, engaging in persistent practice in a discipline, and so on.

The Curriculum of Identity, also stemming from and extending the Core Curriculum, guides students in exploring what practitioners and contributors in disciplines think about; examining how the expert ways of working are interesting, revealing, intriguing, or distasteful to them; developing a sense of themselves as contributors to the chain of human knowledge; examining their own ethics in light of ethical issues presented in the discipline; and so on. AID that is applied to the Curriculum of Identity thus asks students to reflect persistently or deeply on truths, beliefs, ways of working, and styles that typify the field; understand and learn from paradoxes in the field; engage in long-term problem solving on an intractable problem in the field as a means of understanding both the problem and oneself; look for contrasts or comparisons between one's own blind spots, assumptions, and prejudices and those that exist in the field; and so on.

In short, AID as applied to the four parallels in the PCM helps learners continually advance in their capacities to fully realize the intent of the various parallels as they become more like experts in the ways they understand and pursue a discipline. In that way, challenge changes shape to reflect the evolving perspectives a student develops by looking at knowledge through four lenses rather than through a single lens.

USING ASCENDING INTELLECTUAL DEMAND TO PLAN CURRICULUM AND INSTRUCTION

Up to this point, we've established three insights about the concept of AID. First, AID is an approach to providing escalating challenge for learners as they demonstrate readiness for such challenge. Second, AID will focus challenge on increasingly expertlike knowledge, understanding, skill, and behavior. Third, AID will reflect and intensify the unique learning goals of the four parallels in the PCM.

While these three insights are helpful in establishing a sense of the intent of AID, they are not altogether useful in understanding what a teacher would actually do to promote AID in the classroom. Teachers and other curriculum designers and developers will need more specific guidance in how to translate these three broad guidelines into classroom practice. To that end, we suggest four ways of planning for AID in curricular plans.

It is critical to understand that all of these approaches are heuristics, not algorithms. That is, they provide guidance, but not recipes, for teachers. The teacher must work to understand the intent of the guidance, the nature of tasks at hand, and the developmental nature of particular students, crafting the guidance to address requirements of the tasks and needs of students.

Asking Students to Work Like Experts

One option for teachers who want to apply AID for students who are advancing in knowledge, understanding, and skills is simply to ask, "What are the traits and skills of experts across fields?" With some of those general attributes in mind, a teacher can craft instruction in ways that call on students to reflect upon and use those traits and skills. Figure 5.2 draws on some of the more generic hallmarks of experts in a variety of fields (Tomlinson et al., 2002) to establish some directions teachers might ask advanced learners to take in their work to achieve challenge that is both appropriate and increasingly expertlike.

How a teacher adapts the language reflected in Figure 5.2 for particular students will, of course, depend on the development of the student and the task at hand. Take, for example, the capacity to detect relevant information in seemingly extraneous information. One teacher might provide a very bright second grader with four books on animal adaptation, asking that student to find patterns in the animal world that could be useful to humans who have a need to protect themselves. Another teacher might ask a very advanced high school science student to quickly find several Web sites that would be most helpful to peers in formulating a hypothesis about ways in which humans might most efficiently and effectively draw on animal adaptation to address current or future challenges to human survival. Both tasks call on the learner to practice what experts do—understand key features of a problem and find

Figure 5.2   Asking Students to Work Toward Traits and Skills of Experts

- Spend time to lay foundations and understand contexts and problems
- Engage others in reflective, insightful dialogue to solve problems and gather data
- Seek multiple relevant resources for understanding
- Glean pertinent information from seemingly extraneous data
- Pose insightful questions about content and ways of working
- Organize knowledge to enhance meaning and accessibility
- Detect differences in typical and novel instances
- Transfer knowledge and skill from familiar to unfamiliar contexts
- Look for patterns in data
- Represent problems in a thoughtful, productive way
- Step outside personal experience to seek alternative views
- Make useful connections among ideas
- Make more connections and more complex connections among ideas/events
- Create novel (i.e., fresh, unexpected, and useful) applications and products
- Develop systems for effective, efficient learning and problem solving
- Look for and recount significance of events
- Reflect on own thinking and its effectiveness in given situations
- Look for subtle examples and illustrations
- Work at high levels of abstract, analytical, and creative thinking
- Demonstrate high curiosity
- Seek understanding of topic at a deep level
- Raise questions about reasons for and use of knowledge
- Work hard—inspire self to work
- Demonstrate firm commitment to excellence
- Seek meaningful critique
- Work for insights
- Use present knowledge to plan for future directions in learning
- Examine impact of decisions on self, others, and society

information relevant to solving the problem in the midst of less useful information. The sophistication of the task changes as the sophistication of the learner evolves. In other words, the prompts in Figure 5.2 could be useful to advanced learners at all ages. It is the role of the teacher to adapt a particular prompt in response to learner need and task requirement.

Asking Students to Work Like Experts in Specific Disciplines

Although the previous approach to guiding challenge looks at expertise in a more generic fashion by examining general traits of experts in many fields, it is also helpful to look at expertise through the lens of a particular discipline. For example, what specific knowledge, skills, understandings, attitudes, and behaviors typify an expert in mathematics? With such discipline-specific understandings, a teacher can both trace the development of students and coach students to extend that development.

Kelly Hedrick from the Virginia Beach City Public Schools in Virginia has developed a very useful heuristic or guide for thinking about developing expertise in science, math, social studies, and language arts. She began, as the previous section suggests, by mapping how students might progress in more generic terms from Novice to Apprentice to Practitioner to Expert in Knowledge, Skills, Attitudes, and Habits of Mind (see Figure 5.3). It is important to note that the arrows in Figure 5.3

Figure 5.3   Novice to Expert Continuum

Ascending Intellectual Demand

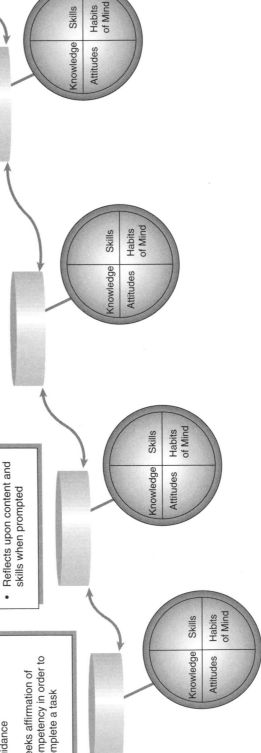

Expert

- Utilizes concepts within and among disciplines in order to derive theories and principles
- Creates innovations within a field
- Practices skill development independently and for the purpose of improvement
- Seeks input from other experts in a field for a specific purpose
- Works to achieve flow and derives pleasure from the experience (high challenge, advanced skill/knowledge)
- Is independent and self-directed as a learner
- Seeks experiences that cause a return to previous levels in varying degrees

Practitioner

- Manipulates two or more microconcepts simultaneously
- Creates generalizations that explain connections among concepts
- Selects and utilizes skills in order to complete a task
- Seeks input from others as needed
- Exhibits task commitment and persistence when challenges are moderate
- Reflects upon both content and skills in order to improve understanding/performance

Apprentice

- Understands the connections among micro-concepts within a discipline
- Connects information within a microconcept
- Begins to interpret generalizations and themes that connect concepts
- Applies skills with limited supervision
- Seeks confirmation at the end of a task
- Reflects upon content and skills when prompted

Novice

- Experiences content at a concrete level
- Manipulates micro-concepts one at a time
- Needs skill instruction and guided practice
- Requires support, encouragement, and guidance
- Seeks affirmation of competency in order to complete a task

Knowledge | Skills
Attitudes | Habits of Mind

and the others that follow indicate a forward-and-backward movement. It is likely the case for most of us that we do not develop in a forward, linear fashion only. As we encounter more complex problems, new ideas or skills, or even difficult times in our personal lives, we need to retrace our developmental steps in order to secure grounding to move ahead again. Nonetheless, it is a very helpful approach to AID to develop a somewhat concrete language and progression of skills for teachers, who can then, in turn, use them to study and guide the development of learners in progression toward expertise.

Figure 5.4 is related to Figure 5.3 and suggests that, if a learner seems currently to be functioning at a Novice level on Figure 5.3 at a given time, then it would be helpful for the teacher to respond with tasks crafted at a Novice level (Figure 5.4). In other words, whereas Figure 5.3 is diagnostic of student development, Figure 5.4 is prescriptive and indicates to teachers some potentially appropriate responses to student development.

Hedrick then moved from the more generic conceptions in Figures 5.3 and 5.4 to discipline-specific applications to science (Figure 5.5), mathematics (Figure 5.6), history (Figure 5.7), and English language arts (Figure 5.8). In each instance, she drew upon national standards documents as she developed the guides. Again in each instance, arrows indicate that learners will inevitably grow in ways that call for retracing of steps, revisiting ideas, and reconsolidating skills even as they move forward toward expertise.

The conceptions represented in Figures 5.3 to 5.8 have great value for a broad range of teachers in both assessing student growth and planning for AID. It would also make sense for other experts in these disciplines to modify the heuristics based on national and local discipline-specific standards and the needs of advancing learners in those locales. Certainly it would be both possible and helpful to develop similar diagnostic and prescriptive guides in the full range of school subjects.

Asking Students to Address Prompts Leading to Ascending Intellectual Demand

While the previous two avenues to AID stress movement toward expertise, an alternate approach stresses challenge via an intensified focus on the intent of the four parallels in the PCM. *The Parallel Curriculum* (Tomlinson et al., 2002) offers specific prompts likely to serve as catalysts for AID in each of the parallels. Those prompts for the Core Curriculum parallel follow here in Figure 5.9, Curriculum of Connections parallel in Figure 5.10, Curriculum of Practice parallel in Figure 5.11, and Curriculum of Identity parallel in Figure 5.12.

Through the use of these and similar prompts, a teacher can guide AID by helping students intensify or extend the particular intent of the four parallel approaches to curriculum design and development in the PCM. As is always the case, the teacher will need to recraft the language of the prompt to address the development of a particular student and the requirements of a particular task. As written, the prompts provide intent, not final student instructions.

(Text continues on page 96)

Figure 5.4 Teacher Response to Student Development of Expertise

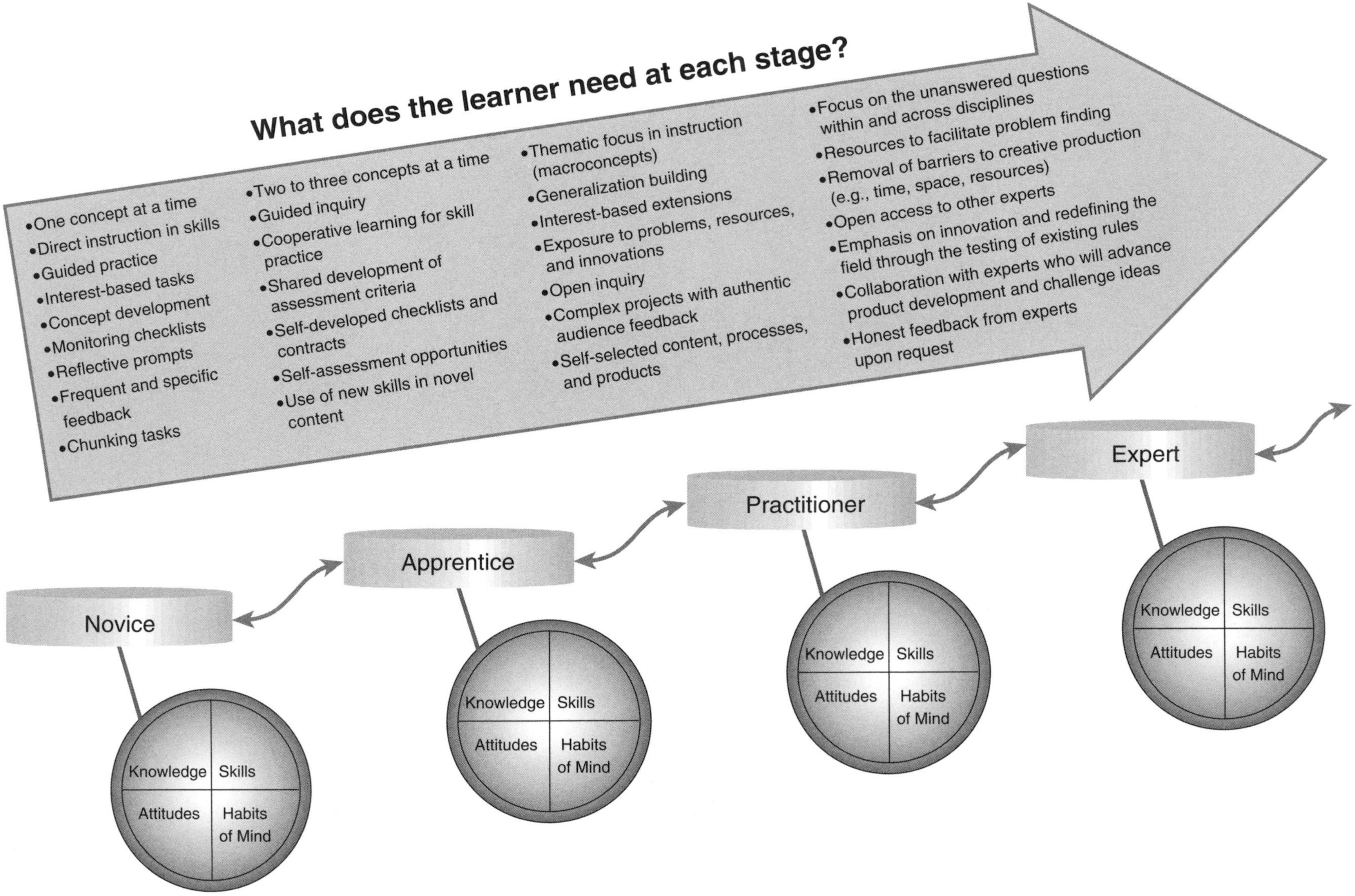
What does the learner need at each stage?
•One concept at a time
•Direct instruction in skills
•Guided practice
•Interest-based tasks
•Concept development
•Monitoring checklists
•Reflective prompts
•Frequent and specific feedback
•Chunking tasks
•Two to three concepts at a time
•Guided inquiry
•Cooperative learning for skill practice
•Shared development of assessment criteria
•Self-developed checklists and contracts
•Self-assessment opportunities
•Use of new skills in novel content
•Thematic focus in instruction (macroconcepts)
•Generalization building
•Interest-based extensions
•Exposure to problems, resources, and innovations
•Open inquiry
•Complex projects with authentic audience feedback
•Self-selected content, processes, and products
•Focus on the unanswered questions within and across disciplines
•Resources to facilitate problem finding
•Removal of barriers to creative production (e.g., time, space, resources)
•Open access to other experts
•Emphasis on innovation and redefining the field through the testing of existing rules
•Collaboration with experts who will advance product development and challenge ideas
•Honest feedback from experts upon request
Novice
Knowledge
Skills
Attitudes
Habits of Mind
Apprentice
Knowledge
Skills
Attitudes
Habits of Mind
Practitioner
Knowledge
Skills
Attitudes
Habits of Mind
Expert
Knowledge
Skills
Attitudes
Habits of Mind

Figure 5.5 Novice to Expert Continuum in Science

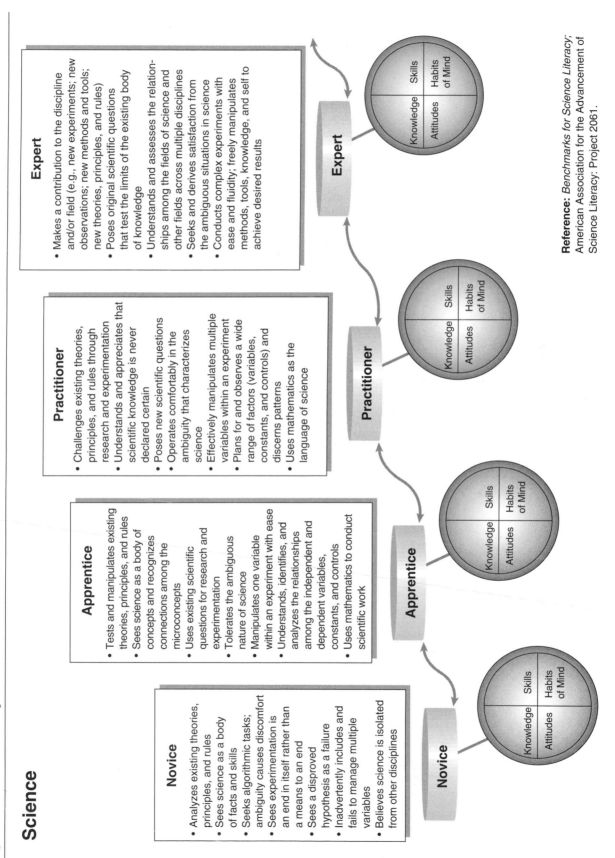

Science

Novice
- Analyzes existing theories, principles, and rules
- Sees science as a body of facts and skills
- Seeks algorithmic tasks; ambiguity causes discomfort
- Sees experimentation is an end in itself rather than a means to an end
- Sees a disproved hypothesis as a failure
- Inadvertently includes and fails to manage multiple variables
- Believes science is isolated from other disciplines

Apprentice
- Tests and manipulates existing theories, principles, and rules
- Sees science as a body of concepts and recognizes connections among the microconcepts
- Uses existing scientific questions for research and experimentation
- Tolerates the ambiguous nature of science
- Manipulates one variable within an experiment with ease
- Understands, identifies, and analyzes the relationships among the independent and dependent variables, constants, and controls
- Uses mathematics to conduct scientific work

Practitioner
- Challenges existing theories, principles, and rules through research and experimentation
- Understands and appreciates that scientific knowledge is never declared certain
- Poses new scientific questions
- Operates comfortably in the ambiguity that characterizes science
- Effectively manipulates multiple variables within an experiment
- Plans for and observes a wide range of factors (variables, constants, and controls) and discerns patterns
- Uses mathematics as the language of science

Expert
- Makes a contribution to the discipline and/or field (e.g., new experiments; new observations; new methods and tools; new theories, principles, and rules)
- Poses original scientific questions that test the limits of the existing body of knowledge
- Understands and assesses the relationships among the fields of science and other fields across multiple disciplines
- Seeks and derives satisfaction from the ambiguous situations in science
- Conducts complex experiments with ease and fluidity; freely manipulates methods, tools, knowledge, and self to achieve desired results

Reference: *Benchmarks for Science Literacy*, American Association for the Advancement of Science Literacy: Project 2061.

Figure 5.6 Novice to Expert Continuum in History

History

Novice

- Defines history as isolated people, places, and events
- Sees the facts and skills, but not the concepts that link them
- Studies history through rote memorization
- Needs experiences with sequencing to establish a sense of chronology
- Identifies causes and effects as isolated events
- Lacks an appreciation for history and its relevance to self and the world in the present and the future

Apprentice

- Understands history at the conceptual level
- Seeks connections among microconcepts in order to make sense of historical patterns and trends
- Poses historical research questions
- Has a clearly defined sense of chronology
- Understands the complexity of causes and effects
- Recognizes the importance of perspective in historical events, human perspectives, and consequences

Practitioner

- Analyzes contemporary events through a historical lens with automaticity
- Understands chronology, but has the ability to follow themes across events and time periods regardless of the direction (present to past, past to present)
- Identifies unanswered questions and crafts researchable questions to investigate them
- Understands the social, political, economic, and technological influences on patterns and trends
- Understands and appreciates the influence of individual experiences, societal values, and traditions on historical perspectives

Expert

- Moves easily from the theoretical to the practical and vice versa in response to a situation
- Challenges accepted bodies of knowledge, methods, and research findings
- Develops themes and connections across historical events, periods, and fields without reliance on but acknowledgment of chronology
- Uses the knowledge and skills of the discipline across diverse fields and disciplines
- Displays curiosity and seeks challenge through unanswered questions in the field
- Marvels at the richness of history and its importance in shaping the present and future
- Systematically and with automaticity utilizes the knowledge, skills, and processes of the discipline to investigate

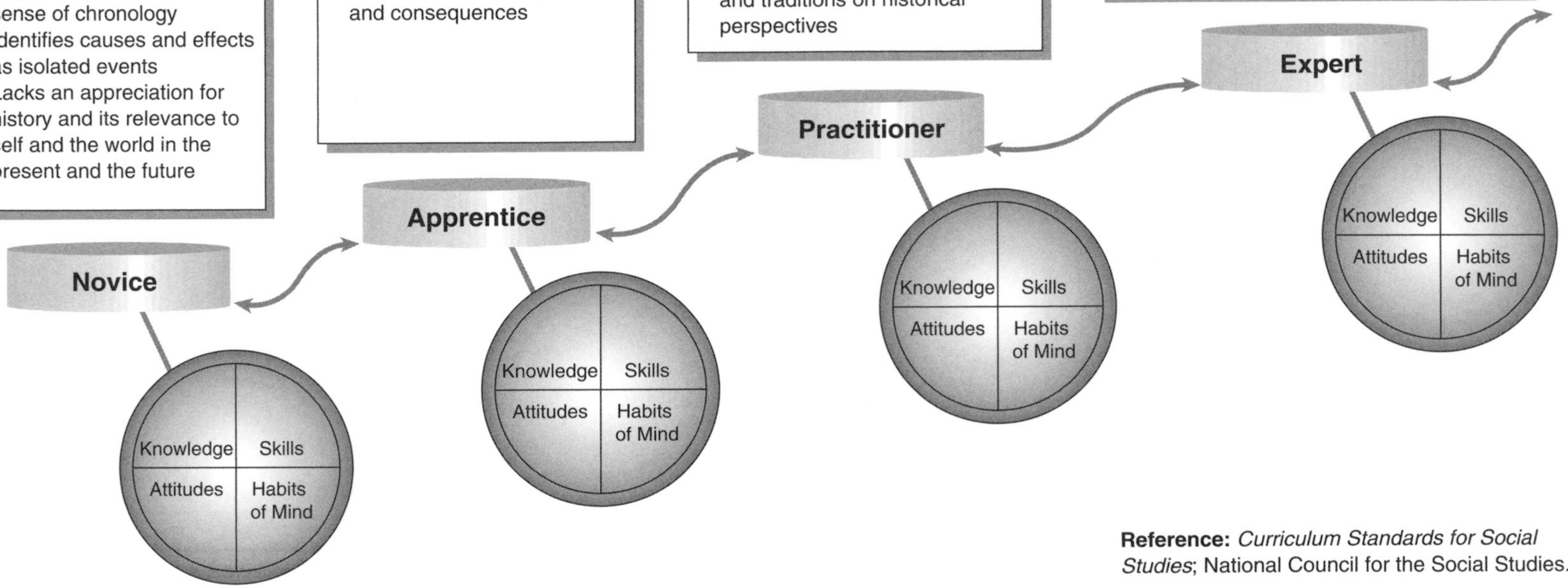

Novice → **Apprentice** → **Practitioner** → **Expert**

(Spheres showing: Knowledge | Skills / Attitudes | Habits of Mind)

Reference: *Curriculum Standards for Social Studies*; National Council for the Social Studies.

Figure 5.7 Novice to Expert Continuum in English Language Arts

English Language Arts

Expert

- Demonstrates knowledge, reflection, creativity, and critical analysis of language arts skills and concepts across a wide variety of disciplines
- Applies the wide range of skills associated with effective oral and written communication, reading, and research with automaticity
- Reading, writing, speaking, and researching lead to personal fulfillment beyond the goals of learning and the exchange of information
- Appreciates the power of the written and spoken word
- Questions the accepted conventions and rules
- Experiments with methods to communicate and develop greater understanding
- Practices in all areas (i.e., written and oral communication, reading, and research)

Practitioner

- Applies the skills of language arts in other disciplines with relative ease
- Moves fluidly among the various modes and methodologies associated with language arts
- Appreciates the art of communication
- Conducts authentic research applying the skills of questioning, information gathering, data analysis, and synthesis
- Understands the necessity for multiple and varied resources in research
- Seeks the constructive criticism of knowledgeable persons across disciplines in developing a product
- Understands and respects the diversity of language across cultures

Apprentice

- Demonstrates flexibility in the use of skills and the understanding of concepts
- Understands the connections across written and oral communication, reading, and research
- Understands the need for a variety of selections in reading, writing, and research
- Understands the role of effective communication for a variety of purposes
- Adjusts communication modes according to purpose and audience
- Values the input of qualified reviewers in the editing and revision process

Novice

- Applies a limited range of skills in an algorithmic manner
- Understands the skills and concepts in isolation, but lacks flexibility in understanding and application
- Practices and applies skills when prompted
- Limits reading selections and resources to a narrow scope
- Written and oral communication is technically correct, but lacks variety and personal relevance
- Sees written and oral communication and research with limited possibilities
- Views editing and revision as punishment and drudgery

Expert — Knowledge / Skills / Attitudes / Habits of Mind

Practitioner — Knowledge / Skills / Attitudes / Habits of Mind

Apprentice — Knowledge / Skills / Attitudes / Habits of Mind

Novice — Knowledge / Skills / Attitudes / Habits of Mind

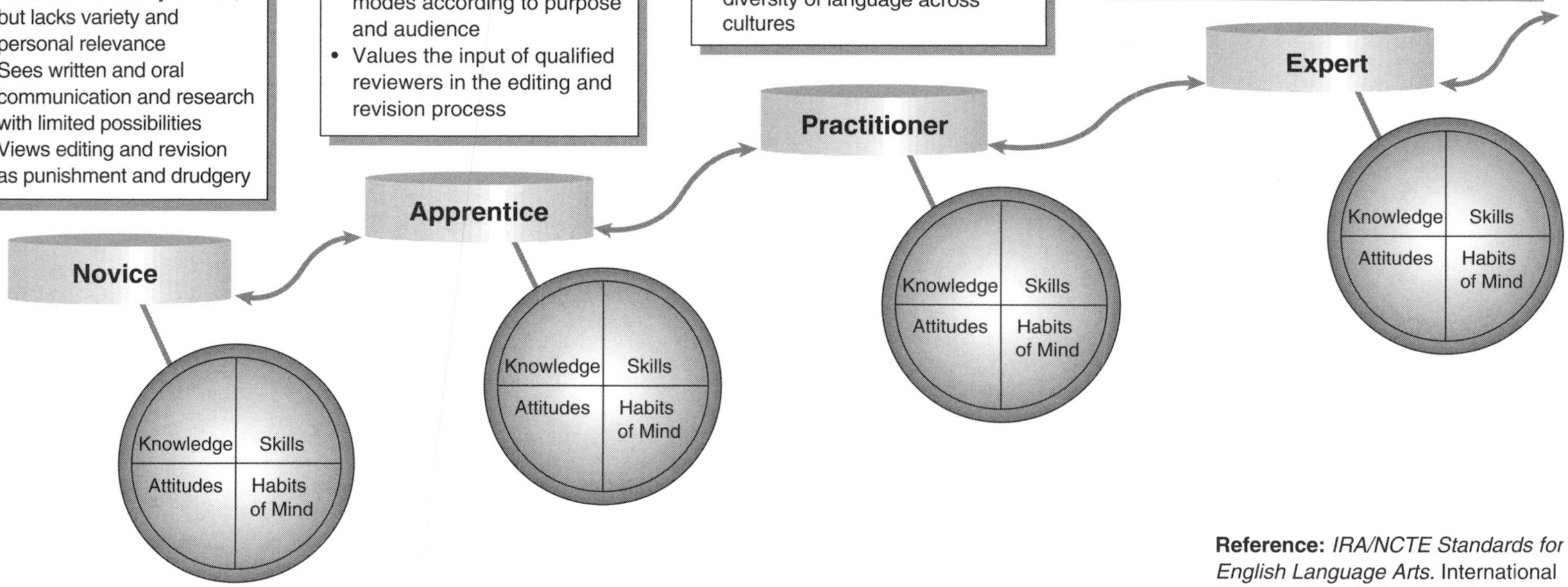

Reference: *IRA/NCTE Standards for English Language Arts.* International Reading Association (2004).

Figure 5.8 Novice to Expert Continuum in Mathematics

Mathematics

Novice

- Applies the skills of discrete mathematics, but lacks a conceptual understanding
- Identifies the principles, but cannot apply them unless prompted
- Computes efficiently, but lacks fluency
- Sees limited relationships among numbers and number systems
- Identifies only the most basic patterns
- Needs frequent feedback and assurance during problem solving
- Sees the "right answer" as the goal

Apprentice

- Connects the relationships among mathematical facts and skills through concepts
- Computes fluently and makes reasonable estimates
- Applies skills with confidence and develops greater understanding beyond number and operations
- Makes connections across mathematical ideas
- Understands the principles that frame a field (i.e., measurement, algebra, geometry, statistics)
- Develops skills and understanding through complex problem solving
- Sets goals that extend beyond computational accuracy

Practitioner

- Uses the principles of mathematics to make connections among concepts across multiple fields within mathematics
- Makes appropriate selections about which tools and methods to use
- Understands patterns, relations, and functions
- Applies skills with automaticity
- Understands change in a variety of contexts
- Uses a variety of tools and methods with efficiency in the analysis of mathematical situations
- Appreciates the role of mathematics in other disciplines
- Formulates questions for research that can be addressed through one or more fields of mathematics

Expert

- Uses computation as merely a means to an end
- Questions existing mathematical principles
- Moves easily among the fields of mathematics through the use of macroconcepts
- Links mathematical principles to other fields through real-world problems
- Seeks the challenge of unresolved problems and the testing of existing theories
- Seeks flow through the manipulation of tools and methods in complex problem solving
- Views unanswered questions in other disciplines through the concepts of mathematics
- Uses reflection and practice as tools for self-improvement

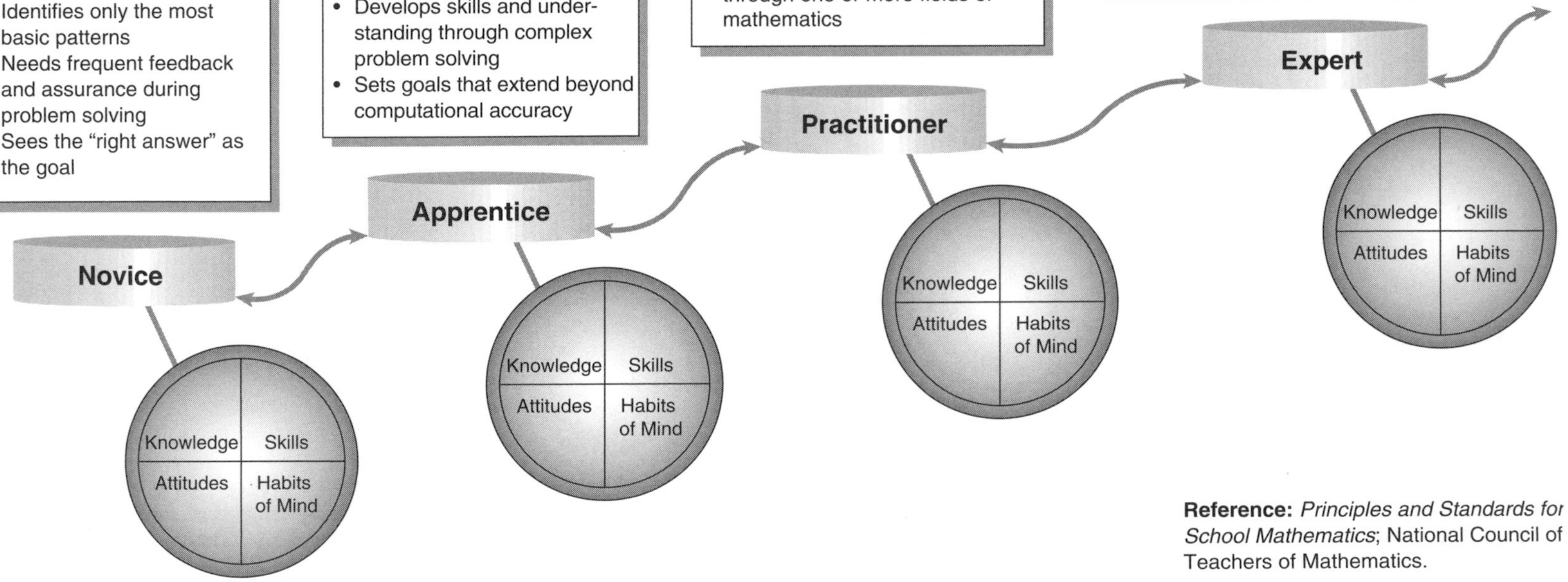
Novice
Knowledge
Skills
Attitudes
Habits of Mind
Apprentice
Knowledge
Skills
Attitudes
Habits of Mind
Practitioner
Knowledge
Skills
Attitudes
Habits of Mind
Expert
Knowledge
Skills
Attitudes
Habits of Mind

Reference: *Principles and Standards for School Mathematics*; National Council of Teachers of Mathematics.

Figure 5.9 Prompts Leading to Ascending Intellectual Demand in the Core Curriculum

- Call on students to use more advanced reading, resources, and research materials.
- Assist students in determining and understanding multiple perspectives on issues and problems.
- Adjust the pace of teaching and learning to account for rapid speed of learning or to permit additional depth of inquiry.
- Develop tasks and products that call on students to work at greater levels of depth, breadth, complexity, or abstraction.
- Have students apply what they are learning to contexts that are unfamiliar or are quite dissimilar from applications explored in class.
- Design tasks and products that are more open ended or ambiguous in nature and/or that call on students to exercise greater levels of independence in thought and scholarly behavior as learners and producers.
- Develop rubrics for tasks and products that delineate levels of quality that include expert-level indicators.
- Encourage collaborations between students and adult experts in an area of shared interest.
- Design tasks that require continuing student reflection on the significance of ideas and information and cause students to generate new and useful methods and procedures to represent ideas and solutions.
- Include directions and procedures that ask students to establish criteria for high-quality work, assess their progress in working toward those criteria, and seek and use feedback that improves their quality of efforts and methods of working.
- Ask students to reflect on the personal and societal implications of solutions they propose to problems.

Figure 5.10 Prompts Leading to Ascending Intellectual Demand in the Curriculum of Connections

- Increase the unfamiliarity of the context or problem in which understandings or skills are applied.
- Ask students to generate defensible criteria against which they then weigh diverse perspectives on a problem or solution (or use professional criteria for the same purpose).
- Call on students to develop solutions, proposals, or approaches that effectively bridge differences in perspective but still effectively address the problem.
- Ask students to make proposals or predictions for future directions based on student-generated, discipline-related patterns from the past in a particular domain.
- Have students search for legitimate and useful connections among seemingly disparate elements (e.g., music and medicine or law and geography).
- Develop tasks or products that seek patterns of interaction among multiple areas (e.g., ways in which geography, economics, politics, and technology affect one another).
- Call on students to look at broad swaths of the world through a perspective quite unlike their own (e.g., how a peer from a culture and economy very different from the student's would react to the student's house, slang, religion, clothing, music, relationships with adults, toys or gadgets, plans for the future, etc.).
- Develop tasks and products that seek out unstated assumptions beneath the surface of beliefs, decisions, approaches, or perspectives.
- Ask students to develop systems for making connections, drawing generalizations, achieving balanced perspectives, or addressing problems.
- Design criteria for students' work that call for a higher standard of quality (such as insightful, highly illustrative, highly synthetic, unusually articulate or expressive, etc.) as opposed to a less demanding but still positive standard of quality (such as appropriate, accurate, feasible, informed, defensible, etc.).

Figure 5.11 Prompts Leading to Ascending Intellectual Demand in the Curriculum of Practice

- Encourage students to distinguish between approaches that seem relevant in tackling authentic problems of the discipline and those that are less relevant.
- Call on students to develop a language of reflection about problems and scenarios in the field.
- Devise tasks and products that cause students to develop, through application, personal frameworks of knowledge, understanding, and skill related to the discipline.
- Have students test those frameworks through repeated field-based tasks and refine them as necessary.
- Have students compare standards of quality used by practitioners, connoisseurs, and critics in the field to standards of quality typically used in school as they relate to problem solving in that field.
- Guide students in establishing their own goals for work at what they believe to be the next steps in quality for their own growth and to assess their own work according to those standards.
- Make it possible for students to submit best-quality exemplars of their own work to experts in a field for expert-level feedback.
- Have students work on problems currently posing difficulties for experts in the discipline.
- Structure products and tasks to require students to engage in persistent, prolonged, and written reflection about their own work and thinking in the field, with analysis and critique of those patterns as they evolve.
- Call on students to compare and contrast their own approaches to discipline-based dilemmas, issues, or problems with those of experts in the field.

Figure 5.12 Prompts Leading to Ascending Intellectual Demand in the Curriculum of Identity

- Look for and reflect on "truths," beliefs, ways of working, styles, and so on that typify the field.
- Look for "roots" of theories, beliefs, and principles in a field and relate those theories, beliefs, and principles to the time when they "took root" in one's own life.
- Look for and reflect on the meaning of paradoxes and contradictions in the discipline or field.
- Conduct an ethnography of a facet of the discipline and reflect on both findings and personal revelations.
- Engage in long-term problem solving on an intractable problem in the discipline that causes the student to encounter and mediate multiple points of view and reflect systematically on the experience.
- Research and establish standards of quality work as defined by the discipline, applying those standards to the student's own work in the discipline over an extended time period and reflecting systematically on the experience.
- Collaborate with a high-level professional or practitioner in the field in shared problem solving and reflection.
- Challenge or look for limitations of the ideas, models, ways of working, or belief systems of the discipline.
- Look for parallels (or contrasts) among personal prejudices, blind spots, assumptions, habits, and those evident in the field.
- Study and reflect on one discipline by using the concepts, principles, and modes of working of another discipline, reflecting on the interactions and insights gained.

Combining Approaches to Ascending Intellectual Demand

Recall that the PCM focuses on challenge through progression toward expertise or through intensification of the goals of the various parallels in the model. Certainly it would often be the case that a teacher would want to combine these avenues to promote student challenge. In other words, in a particular product assignment or in a particular rubric, a teacher might incorporate guidelines asking students to find effective ways to represent the problem on which they are working (e.g., generic traits of experts), to manipulate multiple variables in the problem (e.g., subject-specific trait of experts in science), and to demonstrate how their own framework of understanding the topic evolves as they develop their product (e.g., AID prompt from the Curriculum of Practice).

A teacher who is eager to support student growth can continually draw from, expand on, and combine the three approaches to determining student need and developing curriculum and instruction that supports AID. In such settings, it is likely that both the student and the teacher will grow in capacity to understand and think about critical ideas in more multidimensional and transformational ways.

WHEN AND WHERE DO TEACHERS APPLY ASCENDING INTELLECTUAL DEMAND?

The concept of AID calls on teachers to study and reflect on student development and then to respond in ways likely to challenge the individual learner to develop toward expertlike and ultimately expert-level knowledge, understanding, skills, attitudes, and behaviors. Thus, AID implies both assessment of student growth and response to that growth.

Teachers can use the three avenues suggested earlier for achieving AID as tools for monitoring student development. In so doing, the teacher reflects on what a student can currently accomplish with appropriate effort and support. In other words, the teacher monitors what we might call Continuous Intellectual Ascent. For instance,

- What is the degree of the student's knowledge?
- To what degree is the student imitative or nonimitative in applying knowledge to solve problems?
- What sorts of pattern recognition has the student achieved?
- In what ways is the student working to organize knowledge efficiently and meaningfully?
- How effectively does the student question ideas and generate insights and insightful questions about what he or she is learning?
- To what degree does the student demonstrate growing curiosity, reflection, and concentration?
- How responsible is the student for his or her own work?
- To what extent does the student engage in reflective and evaluative behavior?

As the student demonstrates continuous intellectual ascent, the teacher then seeks to promote and support AID, for example, by

- using more heuristic and fewer algorithmic approaches to problem solving;
- transferring content and skill to use in increasingly novel and unfamiliar contexts;

- working at higher degrees of abstract, critical, and creative thinking;
- using more complex and extensive knowledge and skill;
- searching for more subtle examples;
- seeking more global applicability of principles;
- presenting to more sophisticated audiences;
- honing skills of self-reflection; and
- tolerating greater intellectual risk.

The question of where in the teaching/learning sequence teachers can promote AID has an almost unlimited number of answers. Almost anything a teacher does while teaching and almost anything a learner does while pursuing or expressing knowledge, understanding, and skill can be crafted in ways that extend the student's reach. Among the myriad of options for applying the concept of AID are the following:

- Preassessment
- Ongoing or in-process assessment
- Summative assessment
- Observational checklists
- Product design
- Oral questions for classroom discussion
- Questions for small group discussion
- Journal prompts
- Homework assignments
- Class activities and assignments of all varieties
- Independent studies
- Interest-based tasks or investigations
- WebQuests or Web inquiries
- Research designs
- Rubrics to guide quality of work
- Feedback on student work and performances
- Goal setting in student conferences

A WORD OF CAUTION

It is important to note four areas requiring attention if the concept of AID is to be of maximum value in developing the advancing capacities of students—including those who demonstrate advanced capacity at an earlier time than anticipated in school and at greater degrees of advancement. These four cautions stem from observation of educators attempting to use the concept of AID in curriculum development and modification.

- AID is a modification applied to a curriculum. Thus, if the curriculum to which it is applied is weak, the potential of AID is diminished. In a solid Core Curriculum, for example, all students should be working with the conceptual base of a discipline and moving toward expertise. AID should enable students who are ready to intensify their movement toward expertise to do so in the context of a rich, concept-based study. Conversely, applying AID to a drill-and-practice, worksheet-driven curriculum is not likely to support movement toward expertise.

• Not only does curriculum to which AID is applied need to support movement toward expertise through its conceptual base, but also the various learning experiences in the unit need to flow in such a way that they successively guide students in a trajectory toward expertise. The purposefulness of each learning experience must be clear to students and teacher alike. Further, the learning experiences must be cumulative in their impact. A series of disjointed—even if fun and clever—activities do not support the concept of AID.

• It is important to draw upon standards at multiple grade levels in developing curriculum that will support AID. Effective standards spiral in their complexity across grade levels. At a given moment, some students in a class may need to focus on an iteration of a standard that allows more foundational exploration and application of a principle or skill. For those students, insistence on a "grade-level" standard may exacerbate a gap in understanding rather than span it. Similarly, students ready for AID at an advanced level will likely need to be directed to work with a more advanced iteration of a standard in order to progress further toward expertise.

• To maximize the potential of AID, both curricular units and AID should be planned for in a K–12 scope and sequence of curriculum. Although excellent teachers adapt such sequences to the needs of particular groups and individuals, planning for both a coherent exploration of the disciplines over time and a reasoned progression toward expertise would greatly enhance the likelihood of student development in expertlike and expert-level pathways.

WHY DOES ASCENDING INTELLECTUAL DEMAND MATTER?

In the end, whenever and wherever it is used, the goal of AID replicates the goal of the excellent coach who carefully maps the growth of an athlete and who presents and supports opportunities to develop competencies at ever higher levels of expectation with the desire to help the young person continually develop his or her capacity as an athlete, his or her sense of self-efficacy as an athlete, and his or her readiness to test and hone skills at increasing levels of proficiency.

To become what one ought to be is perhaps the ultimate satisfaction in life. The concept of AID positions all learners to achieve that satisfaction by helping them systematically develop their capacities. AID helps many highly able learners develop good stewardship of their "opportunity of talent." Good stewardship of advanced ability is *not* about

- rote memorization of more information;
- finishing first, or even finishing;
- being given the option to explore or have fun by demonstrating mastery of basics;
- recognition by virtue of norm-based "excellence";

- being sure or being right;
- comfort; or
- hunger for reward.

Good stewardship of advanced ability or the "opportunity of talent," *is* about

- an ongoing quest for understanding, for meaning making;
- a quest for depth of understanding in areas of ability;
- satisfaction derived from self-testing and idea testing;
- persistence;
- continual push for improvement;
- search for open-mindedness, truth, and insight;
- hard work and disciplined work;
- hunger to be productive, to be useful, to push the boundaries of one's own possibilities; and
- guiding others in becoming who and what they might be.

We invite all educators who believe they have a stake in maximizing the capacities in all learners—including those whose reach may already exceed our own—to extend their own reach and that of their students by continuing to study, apply, and expand upon the concept of AID.

Bibliography

(Books 1 and 2 Combined)

Albom, M. (1997). *Tuesdays with Morrie: An old man, a young man, and life's greatest lesson*. New York: Doubleday.

American Association for the Advancement of Science. (1993). *Benchmarks for science literacy*. Oxford, UK: Oxford University Press.

Ammeson, J. (2002, January). The lens of time. *Northwest Airlines World Traveler, 34*(1), 38–43.

The @rtroom, www.arts.ufl.edu/art/rt_room/index.html

Arts EdNet. (1999). *National standards for visual arts education*. Retrieved December 5, 2004, from www.getty.edu/artsednet/resources/Scope/Standards/national.html

Bandura, A. (1993). Perceived self-efficacy in cognitive development and functioning. *Educational Psychologist, 28*, 117–148.

Barton, E. (1997). *Peppe the lamplighter*. New York: HarperTrophy.

Berriault, G. (2002). *Stone boy by Gina Berriault in "The Stone Boy": A Study Guide from Gale's "Short Stories for Students"* (Vol. 7, Chapter 15). Farmington Hills, MI: Thompson Gale.

Betts, G. (1985). *Autonomous learner model for the gifted and talented*. Greeley, CO: Autonomous Learning.

Bloom, B. S. (1956). *Taxonomy of educational objectives: Handbook 1. The cognitive domain*. New York: David McKay.

Bransford, J. D., Brown, A. L., & Cocking, R. R. (2000). *How people learn: Brain, mind, experience, and school*. Washington, DC: National Academy Press.

Brookhart, C. (1998). *Go figure!* Chicago: Contemporary Books.

Brown, M. W., & Weisgard, L. (Illus.). (1990). *The important book*. New York: Harper Trophy.

Bruner, J. (1977). *The process of education*. Cambridge, MA: Harvard University Press.

Budzinsky, F. K. (1995). "Chemistry on stage": A strategy for integrating science and dramatic arts. *School Science and Mathematics, 95*(8), 406–410.

Burns, D. (1993). *A six-phase model for the explicit teaching of thinking skills*. Storrs: University of Connecticut, National Research Center on the Gifted and Talented.

Burns, K. (Director). (2002). *The civil war*. Alexandria, VA: PBS Home Video.

Chapman, C. S. (2003). *Shelby Foote: A writer's life*. Jackson: University Press of Mississippi.

Clavell, J. (1989). *The children's story . . . But not just for children*. New York: Dell.

Cooney, B. (1999). *Elenore*. New York: Puffin Books.

Creech, S. (2001). *Love that dog*. New York: HarperCollins.

Csikszentimihalyi, M. (1990). *Flow: The psychology of optimal experience*. New York: Harper Perennial.

Dahl, R. A. (2002). *How democratic is the American Constitution?* New Haven, CT: Yale University.

Deci, E., & Ryan, R. M. (1985). *Intrinsic motivation and self-determinism in human behavior.* New York: Plenum.

Dewey, J. (1933). *How we think.* Boston: D. C. Heath.

Divine, D. (Director). (1999). *Monet: Shadow and light.* Los Angeles: Steeplechase Entertainment.

Divine, D. (Director). (1999). *Rembrandt: Fathers and sons.* Los Angeles: Steeplechase Entertainment.

Earhart, S. (2001). *VITAL: Visual impact in teaching and learning.* Charleston, SC: Carolina Art Association.

Educational Web Adventures, www.eduweb.com

Eighmey Ltd. (2005). *Eighmey's think tank.* Retrieved December 5, 2004, from http://kancrn.kckp.k12.ks.us/Harmon/breighm/zog.html

Eighmey Ltd. (2005). *Eighmey's think tank: Reading and understanding a legal case.* Retrieved December 5, 2004, from http://kancrn.kckps.k12.ks.us/Harmon/breighm/case.html

Emory University. (2004). *Amendments never ratified for the U.S. Constitution.* Retrieved December 4, 2004, from www.law.emory.edu/FEDERAL/usconst/notamend.html

Erev, I., & Roth, A. E. (1998). Predicting how people play games: Reinforcement learning in experimental games with unique, mixed strategy equilibria. *The American Economic Review, 88,* 848–881.

Erev, I., & Roth, A. E. (1999). On the role of reinforcement learning in experimental games: The cognitive game-theoretic approach. In D. V. Budescu, I. Erev, & R. Zwick (Eds.), *Games and human behavior: Essays in honor of Amnon Rapoport* (pp. 53–77). Mahwah, NJ: Lawrence Erlbaum Associates.

Erickson, H. (1998). *Concept-based curriculum and instruction: Teaching beyond the facts.* Thousand Oaks, CA: Corwin.

Film Study Center, Harvard University. (n.d.). *DoHistory.* Retrieved December 5, 2004, from www.dohistory.org/

Franchere, R. (1970). *Cesar Chavez.* New York: Crowell.

Franklin Institute Online, http://sln.fi.edu/franklin/statsman/statsman.html

Fritz, J. (2003). On writing biography. In D. E. Norton, S. E. Norton, & A. McClure (Eds.), *Through the eyes of a child: An introduction to children's literature* (6th ed.). Upper Saddle River, NJ: Pearson Education.

Gardner, H. (1993). *Creating minds: An anatomy of creativity seen through the lives of Freud, Einstein, Picasso, Stravinsky, Eliot, Graham, and Gandhi.* New York: Basic Books.

Giraffe Heroes Project. (n.d.). *Welcome to giraffe country.* Retrieved December 5, 2004, from www.giraffe.org/

Glaser, R. (1984). Education and thinking: The role of knowledge. *American Psychologist, 39*(2), 93–104.

Goleman, D. P. (1995). *Emotional intelligence: Why it can matter more than IQ for character, health and lifelong achievement.* New York: Bantam Books.

Gregory, J. M. (1971). *Frederick Douglass, the orator: Containing an account of his life, his eminent public services, his brilliant career as orator, selections from his speeches and writings.* New York: Crowell. Available from http://docsouth.unc.edu/neh/gregory/menu.html

Haines, K. (n.d.). *The exponential growth/decay WebQuest.* Retrieved December 5, 2004, from www.web-and-flow.com/members/khaines/exponents/webquest.htm

Hearn, B. (1997). *Seven brave women.* New York: Greenwillow.

History Matters, www.historymatters.gmu.edu/

Housen, A. (1979). *A review of studies in aesthetic education.* Unpublished manuscript, Harvard Graduate School of Education, Cambridge, MA.

Hughes, L. (1991). *Thank you m'am* (Creative Short Stories). Saint John's, Newfoundland, Canada: Creative Company.

Igus, T. (1992). *When I was little.* East Orange, NY: Just Us Books.

International Reading Association. (2004). *IRA/NCTE standards for the English language arts.* Retrieved December 5, 2004, from www.readwritethink.org/standards/

Irons, P. H. (1990). *The courage of their convictions: Sixteen Americans who fought their way to the Supreme Court.* New York: Penguin Books.

ISTENETS. (2004). *Technology Foundation standards for all students.* Retrieved December 5, 2004, from http://cnets.iste.org/students/s_stands.html

Johnson, S. (1750). *The rambler #60.* Retrieved December 5, 2004, from www.samueljohnson.com/ram60.html

Joyce, J., & and Weil, S. (1996). *Models of teaching.* Boston: Allyn & Bacon.

Kaplan, S. (1994). *Differentiating core curriculum and instruction to provide advanced learning opportunities.* Sacramento: California Association for the Gifted.

Khun, D. (1986). Education for thinking. *Teachers College Record, 87*(4), 495–512.

Knowledge Network Explorer. (2004). *Lessons, WebQuests, information for teachers and librarians.* Retrieved December 5, 2004, from www.kn.pacbell.com/

Kohlberg, L. (1964). Moral education in the schools: A developmental view. *School Review, 74,* 1–29.

Krathwohl, D. R., Bloom, B. S., & Masia, B. B. (1964). *Taxonomy of educational objectives: The classification of educational goals: Handbook 2. Affective domain.* New York: David McKay.

Kunhardt-Davis, E. (1987). *Pompeii . . . Buried alive!* New York: Random House.

Lauber, P. (1998). *Painters of the caves.* Washington, DC: National Geographic Society.

Library of Congress, www.loc.gov/

Library of Congress. (2004). *How to read a poem out loud.* Retrieved December 5, 2004, from www.loc.gov/poetry/180/p180-howtoread.html

Library of Congress. (2004). *Section 2: Analysis of primary sources.* Retrieved December 5, 2004, from http://memory.loc.gov/learn/lessons/psources/analyze.html

Lyon, G. (1992). *Who came down that road?* New York: Orchard Press.

MacKenzie, M. (1995). *Abandonings: Photographs of Otter Tail County, Minnesota.* Washington, DC: Eliott & Clark.

Mahoney, A. (1998). In search of gifted identity: From abstract concept to workable counseling constructs. *Roeper Review, 20*(3), 222–226.

Maker, J., & Nielson, A. (1996). *Curriculum development and teaching strategies for the gifted and talented.* Austin, TX: Pro-Ed.

Montana Heritage Project, www.edheritage.org/

Moser, R. (Director). (1999). *Goya: Awakened in a dream.* Los Angeles: Steeplechase Entertainment.

Moser, R. (Director). (1999). *Mary Cassatt: American impressionist.* Los Angeles: Steeplechase Entertainment.

Nash, G. B., & Crabtree, C. (Project Codirectors). (1994). *National standards for United States history: Exploring the American experience.* Los Angeles: University of California, National Center for History in the Schools.

National Academy of Sciences. (1995). *National science education standards.* Retrieved December 6, 2004, from www.nap.edu/readingroom/books/nses/html/

National Association for Gifted Children. (2000). *The parallel curriculum model: A model for planning curriculum for gifted learners* (Pilot version). Washington, DC: Author.

National Center for History in the Schools. (1996). *National standards for history, Basic edition.* Retrieved December 5, 2004, from http://nchs.ucla.edu/standards/

National Council of Teachers and Mathematics. (2000). *Principles and standards for school mathematics: An overview.* Available from http://standards.nctm.org/document/

National Council for the Social Studies. (2004). *Curriculum standards for social studies: 2. Thematic strands.* Retrieved December 5, 2004, from www.socialstudies.org/standards/strands/

National Research Council. (1999). *How people learn: Brain, mind, experience, and school.* Washington, DC: National Academy Press.

Phenix, P. (1964). *Realms of meaning: A philosophy of the curriculum for general education.* New York: McGraw-Hill.

Plumley, E. (2004). *The exponentials WebQuest.* Retrieved December 5, 2004, from www.web-and-flow.com/members/eplumley/exponentials/webquest.htm

Presseisen, B. Z. (1987). *Thinking skills throughout the curriculum.* Bloomington, IN: Pi Lambda Theta.

Raylman, D. (2004). *The exponentials WebQuest.* Retrieved December 5, 2004, from www.srsd.org/~kcornelius/raylman/webquest.htm

Renzulli, J. S. (2002). Expanding the conception of giftedness to include co-cognitive traits and to promote social capital. *Phi Delta Kappan, 84*(1), 33–58. Retrieved from www.sp.uconn.edu/~nrcgt/sem/expandgt.html

Renzulli, J., Leppien, J., & Hays, T. (2000). *The multiple menu model: A critical guide for developing differentiated curriculum.* Mansfield Center, CT: Creative Learning Press.

Renzulli, J., & Reis, S. (1997). *The schoolwide enrichment model: A how-to guide for educational excellence* (2nd ed.). Mansfield Center, CT: Creative Learning Press.

Roberts, T., & Billings, L. (1998). *The Paideia classroom: Teaching for understanding.* Larchmont, NY: Eye on Education.

Rossetti, C. (1872). *Who has seen the wind?* Available at www.recmusic.org/lieder/r/rossetti/wind.html or http://www.grc.nasa.gov/WWW/K-12/Summer_Training/Elementary97/WhoHasSeenTheWind.html

Roth, A. E., & Erev, I. (1995). Learning in extensive-form games: Experimental data and simple dynamic models in the intermediate term. *Games and Economic Behavior, 8,* 164–212.

Ryan, P. M. (1999). *Amelia and Eleanor go for a ride: Based on a true story.* New York: Hyperion.

Ryan, T. J. (Director). (1999). *Degas: Degas and the dancer.* Los Angeles: Steeplechase Entertainment.

Schaefer, C. L. (2001). *The copper tin cup.* New York: Walker Books.

Schelby, A. (2000). *Homeplace.* New York: Orchard.

Shinew, D. M., & Fischer, J. M. (Eds.). (1997). *Comparative lessons for democracy: A collaborative effort of educators from the Czech Republic, Hungary, Latvia, Poland, Russia, and the United States.* Calabasas, CA: Center for Civic Education in cooperation with Ohio State University.

Smith, G. B., & Smith, A. L. (1992). *You decide: Applying the Bill of Rights to real cases.* Pacific Grove, CA: Critical Thinking Press & Software.

Southern, T., & Jones, E. (1991). *The academic acceleration of gifted children.* New York: Teachers College Press.

Sternberg, R. J. (1985). *Beyond IQ: A triarchic theory of human intelligence.* New York: Cambridge University Press.

Sternberg, R. J., & Grigorenko, E. L. (2000). *Teaching for successful intelligence: To increase student learning and achievement.* Arlington Heights, IL: Skylight.

Strickland, C. A., & Hench, E. (2003, March). *Affective differentiation.* Paper presented at Association for Supervision and Curriculum Development Annual Conference, San Francisco.

Strong, M., & Strong, D. M. (1997). *The habit of thought: From Socratic seminars to Socratic practice.* Tonowanda, NY: New View Publications.

Swartz, R. J. (1994). *Infusing critical and creative thinking into content instruction.* Pacific Grove, CA: Critical Thinking Press & Software.

Tomlinson, C. A. (1996). Good teaching for one and all: Does gifted education have an instructional identity? *Journal for the Education of the Gifted, 20,* 155–174.

Tomlinson, C. A. (1999). *The differentiated classroom: Responding to the needs of all learners.* Alexandria, VA: Association for Supervision and Curriculum Development.

Tomlinson, C. A., Kaplan, S., Renzulli, J., Purcell, J., Leppien, J., & Burns, D. (2002). *The parallel curriculum: A design to develop high potential and challenge high-ability learners.* Thousand Oaks, CA: Corwin.

VanTassel-Baska, J., & Little, C. (Eds.). (2003). *Content-based curriculum for high-ability learners.* Waco, TX: Prufrock Press.

Ward, V. (1980). *Differential education for the gifted.* Ventura, CA: National/State Leadership Training Institute for the Gifted and Talented.

Wenger, E. (1998). *Communities of practice: Learning, meaning, and identity.* Cambridge, MA: Cambridge University Press.

What Kids Can Do, www.whatkids cando.org

Wiggins, G., & McTighe, J. (1998). *Understanding by design.* Alexandria, VA: Association for Supervision and Curriculum Development.

Zeller, B. (2000). *Civil war collection: Artifacts and memorabilia from the war between the states.* San Francisco: Chronicle Books.

Zuo, L., & Cramond, B. (2001). An examination of Terman's children from the theory of identity. *Gifted Child Quarterly, 45,* 251–259.

Index

Page references followed by *fig* indicate an illustrated figure.

**CORWIN
PRESS**

The Corwin Press logo—a raven striding across an open book—represents the union of courage and learning. Corwin Press is committed to improving education for all learners by publishing books and other professional development resources for those serving the field of PreK–12 education. By providing practical, hands-on materials, Corwin Press continues to carry out the promise of its motto: **"Helping Educators Do Their Work Better."**

DATE DUE

GAYLORD

PRINTED IN U.S.A.